SPEAK & LIVE YOUR LEGACY

A book for leaders and entrepreneurs
who want to be successful and meaningful

Amélie Yan-Gouiffes

bubok
EDITORIAL

Amélie Yan-Gouiffes

SPEAK & LIVE YOUR LEGACY

A book for leaders
and entrepreneurs who
want to be successful
and meaningful

© Amélie Yan-Gouiffes
© Speak & Live Your Legacy

ISBN: 978-84-685-4366-6

Edited by Bubok Publishing S.L.
equipo@bubok.com
Tel: 912904 490
C/Vizcaya, 6
28045 Madrid

To Léo-Jules and Louis-Maddox, my sons.

Endorsements

As a person who has travelled the globe and has had varied experiences, Amelie Yan-Gouiffes has written a unique book that is at once eminently readable and useful. The book is written in an authentic, empathic and reflective voice. It avoids the trap of excessive sentimentality and nostalgia.

It is partly a meditation on the human condition and partly a distillation of life lessons.

"Speak and Live Your Legacy" is a breath of fresh air. It doesn't preach. It invites you to embark on an inner journey that will manifest positive changes in your worldly life.

Kamal Kishore
Member (Rank of Secretary to Government), National Disaster Management Authority, Government of India.

A practical book filled with inspiring stories on how to find the rough diamond within you, and how by facing and tackling the challenges of life you can keep on polishing your diamond to optimize its brilliance.

By understanding who you are, who you want to be, and what you will do, you can mindfully craft your own legacy as you journey through life.

Fred Mouawad
Serial entrepreneur, Elite diamantaire,
Founder of Synergia One Group.

I read this book cover to cover as it was difficult for me to put it down. The stories that Amelie tells are full of humanity, kindness and fire. Though most probably not a lot of people can experience the same, all of us can however relate to that feeling of a moment, a person and/or a conversation that leaves an impact in our lives.

This book reminds you to pay more attention and to be more aware to those moments that more often are within our reach.

After reading this book, I feel like I can run a marathon, go on humanitarian missions, talk to random people more but mostly I feel the need to be kinder to myself.

Thank you for your legacy, Amélie.

Anggun
World's best-selling Asian
female recording artist.

So many people are searching for a deep meaning in life, and struggle to find it. In *Speak and Live Your Legacy*, Amelie guides you through her rich stories while she traveled the world, on the right formula to help you create and experience a rich and meaningful life.

Rock Thomas
Speaker, Author & #IAmMovement
Podcaster, RockThomas.com

Index

Foreword

As a reader, I found Amélie Yan-Gouiffes' story-telling a unique and captivating experience. In these days of hardcore messaging, her publication, *Speak and Live Your Legacy*, tells powerful stories of hope and resilience – yet in a soft and simple way. The audience is aimed at leaders and entrepreneurs who want to live successful and meaningful careers, but I believe the stories herein will have an impact and be beneficial for anyone who reads them.

The main point is that there's a 'legacy' diamond in us all – but without recognizing the inner power we have, and the choices we make, that diamond may never shine, and we may never reach our legacies.

She explains that legacies are shaped by the people we meet and with whom we interact throughout our careers. Amélie's stories are about the people she has met, some of whom, even in their most difficult times, were able to pick themselves up and move forward stronger than ever.

I realized, in my own mind, that we need a lot more stories like this in an increasingly complex and dangerous world. We need to celebrate positivity over negativity if our own diamonds are to shine in a way that will help us make the world a better place.

The pages that follow will take you through emotional yet hopeful stories of humanity – and its individual strengths – and how witnessing and remembering your own experiences with people you've met can help you 'speak and live your legacy'.

She writes: "Passivity ejects us from the change leader's seat, which may instigate a change that might not be the kind we want. But action gives us control over change. Action activates our self-esteem and confidence. It tells us that, yes, I am enough to make a difference."

I have met Amelia. She is a woman with a positive spirit and energy. (She is a small woman but has a big presence!).

You can feel her presence even in a crowded room. She is always smiling – a happy presence – and possesses an amazing talent for helping those around her to relax and engage in a comfortable and positive way.

And so, in that sense, these stories are an extension of the author and her talents as a human being. Amélie – more inspirational stories please!

Kundhavi Kadiresan

Kundhavi Kadiresan is a global leader fiercely committed to the development agenda and bringing an innovative and transformative vision. She is originally from India and counts with nearly 30 years of experience in Asia, Africa, Eastern Europe, and Latin America.

Her rich career includes leading high-level policy dialogue and managing large loan portfolios with the World Bank Group as well as the Regional Representation for Asia and the Pacific of the FAO - Food and Agriculture Organisation of the United Nations.

Introduction

"As a business, it is not about empowering ourselves. It is about the legacy we leave to the world for human beings."
Jack Ma

It is Saturday morning ; I am sipping a matcha tea and scrolling through the Harvard Business Review. When I click on *"Put Purpose at the Core of your Strategy"*, I anticipate I am going to find something I like.

Three researchers[1] discuss the best-known strategies to boost maximum growth in companies. For eight years, they studied 28 companies in the United States, Europe and India, which had had an average compound annual growth rate of 30% or more in the past five years. The strategies they identified included: create new markets; serve the largest number of stakeholders' needs; and change the rules of the game.

The researchers knew purpose is nothing new for companies. However, it is usually treated more as a something extra to create shared value, increase motivation and to give back to the community. The great discovery of the study is that the companies exhibiting the most growth had shifted purpose from the periphery of their strategy to its core, resulting in "sustained profitable growth" and helping them to "remain relevant in a world that changes rapidly."

---

1. Thomas W. Malnight, Ivy Buche, Charles Dhanaraj.

We all know that making money for the sake of making money does not constitute a legacy for oneself nor for the world. But making money with a vision and for a greater purpose, one that creates an imprint, *does*. This science-backed demonstration that purpose is essential not just for personal fulfillment but for economic growth makes my heart soar. I wonder how many possibilities and opportunities can result from this change of understanding about the value of purpose and legacy in the business world.

Legacy is the imprint we leave when we meet people at different times and in different areas of our lives, through our presence, our actions and decisions, and living your legacy is what this book is about.

You might be asking: Wait a second, what does it mean to be *living* your legacy? Isn't a legacy something that is left behind? Something to think of during your final days in this world?

The day we depart and look back on our life will be too late. There will be no time left to catch up, to create, or to complete what we have not yet accomplished. That is why, rather than only considering what we are leaving behind, our legacy needs to be what we *live*. Now. When it really counts.

It is today, in this moment, that we crave purpose — something bigger than ourselves, something independent from our background or gender, that fuels our life and business. Something that makes us jump out of bed in the morning, all fired up.

The people that I am going to present to you have left indelible imprints on my life and, after a few pages, they will leave lasting impressions on your life, too, and yet — they don't know it. Many times, we have no idea of the legacy we leave in our wake, thorough simple, significant or great moments. The invitation of this book is to become aware of the marks we leave and to improve our lives and businesses with a clear sense of purpose, helping us maintain the energy, perseverance and creativity necessary for success.

Bronnie Ware, a palliative care worker and the author of "The Top Five Regrets of the Dying," writes that those on their deathbeds most regret not having had the courage to live authentically, according to their true selves. Looking back, they recognize how many of their dreams had gone unfulfilled. And, perhaps worst of all, is to die knowing that this lack of fulfillment was due to the choices we made or the actions we did not take.

It is common for us humans to ignore our gut feelings and live the lives others expect of us instead of the lives we want. But this book is not about how we will feel at the end of our lives. This book is about how to live our legacies today.

Where do we look for purpose? We tend to look for it outside of ourselves. We look with envy at others who seem fulfilled and aligned because their social media statuses say so, or because we always believe others will succeed more than we ever could.

The purpose is closer to us than we think, it is within us, with a part outside our comfort zone. If everything was packaged within our comfort zone, all the people of the world would live in total coherence with their purpose. All entrepreneurs would feel in line with their missions; 100percent of professionals would know why they do their jobs. We know this is not the case and it is because living our legacies means doing things that are sometimes uncomfortable and uncertain, daring to go, think, dream and act outside our world.

It's important to remember, too, that your purpose is not fixed for a lifetime. We are so used to things that can be acquired that purpose seems this one tangible, immutable thing. Something that could perhaps be defined in three words. Something permanent and fixed, but it is not. Purpose is dynamic.

So how can you understand what your purpose is? You'll need to do some inner work and connect within to a place author and coach Alexandra Franzen calls the "huts," a mix of heart and guts. She writes: "Your hut is the voice of instinct and intuition, that inexplicable feeling of what's right for you and you alone. Your hut doesn't always speak in words. Sometimes it speaks in feelings, tingles, an invisible hand on your shoulder, a fire in your belly, tears in your eyes that won't stop."

This is how it felt five years ago, when I decided to quit my day job at the European Union, leave a career that I was passionate about and that was the only thing I knew, to open my own company and explore other ways to serve the world in which I believe.

My gut and heart told me it was the right thing to do. Though there were days when I cried more tears than I thought my body could stand.

In the midst of sorrow, my heart and my guts knew I was at the right place — the place I had to be to experience purpose and create my legacy. I understand today that the call was not that my next step was to become a coach, consultant or speaker as an end in and of itself. The call was for the journey, the exploration, the pain and the adrenaline of expanding and discovering parts of me, parts of my heart, my soul and my mind. This growth would happen by experiencing an entirely different world of work, through the material and spiritual dimension of entrepreneurship .

When did I start enjoying it? Was that when I started making money? Actually, it was well before. I started enjoying when I began to find my purpose in it, when I started to see the impact of the added value I was giving to these entrepreneurs, multinationals and start-ups, when I learnt to be fully myself and to live my own legacy. The novelty, the challenges, the things to learn and the encounters were exciting features.

Your 'huts' will tell you when you are there. Do not get disturbed by the noise of others who may doubt you or grill you with questions. They have no bad intentions, but they are seeking how to get to that place where they find purpose and this experience of "living" their legacy. So, they are looking for reassurance, the one truth, the one box to tick. If they are ready to hear you, explain them how embracing different part of the Self is no threat but, on the contrary, a reward. If they are not, respect their journey, but do not let yourself become doubtful or stop what you have started. Some may not have the courage to step outside their comfort zone and might want to see you back in yours.

Purpose is definitely about others. It is about giving. Giving — this is not a synonym of charity, something I am reminded about today, in Comoros. I am at a lovely French guesthouse and it is raining. I am recalling my first field visit on the island when I met Abdillah Msaidié, who likes to introduce himself with his first and last name to which he adds, "Mtswa Mbe," meaning, "cattle farmer." He is so proud of this title. It takes me our full conversation to understand his "why." He's showing us his losses due to the passage of Hurricane Kenneth end of April 2019 but still his spirits soar. He has lost a quarter of his cattle and seven tons of cattle food and supplements, but his smile does not leave his face. All of him smiles, his words too. What is it? How can he keep smiling in the face of such adversity?

Then he finally says it: The project - a project of the United Nations Development Program - has a component of mutual learning, mentoring and exchange of advice among farmers. For him, this is the main jewel of the program. He is giving to others and contributing. It is not about charity — it is about contribution, the kind that gives purpose and which you materialize through living your legacy.

Satell Institute — a major "Think and Do" tank dedicated to corporate social responsibility (CSR) — has produced many research papers and reports on how CSR impacts talent acquisition and retention. Young talents like to choose where they are going to work, and they want the image of the company to correspond to what they fancy. They require a more sophisticated motivation than to meet their basic needs. And this is where a company's dedication to CSR can impact the ability to recruit and retain the best talents.

CSR also positively affects consumer purchasing behavior. Specifically, CSR activities in the employment development and environmental sustainability domains most effectively attract customers toward specific products and brands.

I can relate to this on both aspects. I like to choose who I work with and the standards of the project with which they want me to get involved. As a consumer, CSR actions or omissions definitely impact my behavior. One example is when I settled in Spain in 2018 and I had to choose a bank. They all offered very similar ranges of services. I chose the one with the most developed CSR offer and the offer that was, to me, the most intelligently developed, an offer that looked more than a marketing product, one that seemed truthful, sincere and impactful. There are a couple of things I am not very fond of in terms of their personal banking services. I confess I am not looking at other banks because I like the idea of being part, as a client, of structured and massive social impact.

Contribution and purpose exist outside charity. Often companies willing to engage into Corporate Social Responsibility (CSR) find a charity that has no links with the mission of the company, its products or services. The customers nor the staff are able to make the link between the ad-hoc activities and their daily missions, and, therefore, the CSR does not fuel up, as much as it could, motivation, commitment and ownership.

Social responsibility is not only corporate, it belongs to each one and begins with the duty to work in it actively; and a very simple way to start it is by living our footprint with more commitment and ambition.

In 22 years of collaborating with humanitarian organisations, I met some employees who work there with no sense of contribution. They are as unhappy as a private sector professional who does not relate their work to their values. Contribution is a need of all of us — a universal need, regardless of cultural, professional or personal backgrounds.

And this is what I invite you to do: To speak and to live your legacy, your contribution — because the world needs it. Because you deserve it. Because your company, your life and your whole being are entitled to harvest the happiness and success it will bring.

Some personalities of the personal development world try to sell us the promise of a life where we are on a high every second of our lives, if only we would be disciplined and apply their formula.

I bought this idea and I tried, for a number of years, to keep the adrenaline over the roof in every moment — never stopping, reaching unprecedented levels of productivity, blaming myself for everything that was not going to plan and filling up my heart with much self-guilt. I succeeded, too. But one day, I was burnt out and lacking purpose, feeling sad, suffering from a brutal episode of anemia and insisting on a relationship that was at the antipodes of my dreams and values. Living our legacy is a path. It is not always a pathway of roses but it always leads to an incredible final destination.

I am now learning to live my legacy with intensity and considering that all of it is not into actions but also presence, values. We have to take care of the instrument we are. I integrate this learning in the pages that follow, in this book that is a hybrid of inspiring stories and workbooks. The legacy corresponds to every moment and, at the same time, it is a path. Not always a pathway of roses, but at all times with an incredible final destination.

This book is no formula. This book is a sharing of experiences and inspirations, of tools that worked for me and for the people I was blessed to work with and to The exercises will help you crystallize the legacy you are living and the next level to which you want to take it. There will be days when you will cry, doubt and fail — and those are parts of the legacy you live, too. The only thing I can guarantee is that the more you are into your contribution, the greater number of happy and successful days you will have. It will also be easier to accept the low days, to learn the lessons needed, and to welcome and enjoy the pains and tears of growth and

There is an urgent need for all to regain resilience and purpose by living according to our true selves with a sense of purpose. It is the only way to leave behind legacies that matter. And the more we speak and live our legacy today, the faster we will co-create a world where we all can be, become and belong in the future.

I am grateful to partner with you on this journey!

Amélie

Chapter 1

COLOMBIA

"We are all called. If you're here breathing, you have a contribution to make to our human community. The real work of your life is to figure out your function — your part in the whole — as soon as possible, and then get about the business of fulfilling it as only you can."
Oprah Winfrey

It's 1999. I am on my second humanitarian mission; this time with the Red Cross. I am flying to the coffee-growing region of Colombia and its prosperous town called Armenia. Before today, I had only seen pictures of coffee plantations, showing their rugged but structured landscapes, packed with different shades of green and lavish coffee bushes with red berries weighing the branches down.

Colorful immense houses, with their hammocks hanging side to side of the porch, and Willy jeeps parked in front. There is an abundance and extravagance of colors, beauty and life. My heart beats fast. My adrenaline level is on a high, like it will be each time I am called to a crisis. I know this is the place I need to be. It is where my mission lies.

A few days ago, on January 25th, an earthquake of an intensity of 6.2 points on the Richter scale impacted the area. When we reach the main affected part of town in the outskirts of the plantations, I can barely see anything except an immense cloud of dust mixed with a thick fog. But now that I step out of the car and walk, I can see destruction.

Not a single house remains. Blocks of cement pile on top of each other in a dangerous balance; electric cables dangle like jungle lianas, water pipes are burst open into the air. You cannot figure out where the streets used to be. The search and rescue teams are still checking and cross-checking for any life to be miraculously extracted from these layers of ruin. Humanitarian workers actively roam around to register the survivors and assess where to set the temporary shelters and the food distribution points.

It is a death-like scene despite the incessant movement of all the people around. I am surrounded by skeletons of mortar that used to be buildings and memories of lives that are not anymore. The fog today is especially mournful - even the sky cannot rejoice.

On a vestige of a wall, I read: "If the Phoenix rose from its ashes, we rise again from the rubble."[2]

The phoenix, the ultimate symbol of strength and renewal, reborn from the ashes of the past arising from the flames as a winner, beating all life's challenges and defeating hard times.

Powerful message that brings tears to my heart and my eyes. It is the first time in my life I am directly viewing the horror of a town erased from the map in few seconds.

The colors of uplifting messages painted on the few surviving walls are the only colors I can see among all this greyish rubble. The scene is surreal and yet so painfully real. The homes are no more, but people stay on their plots of land to make sure their ownership would not be stolen, the last tangible property they hold, the only places they have.

A woman calls out to me with a hand wave, requesting me to come to her. I start walking in her direction

---

2. *Si el ave Fenix se levantó de las cenizas, nosotros nos levantamos de los escombros* – in blue color on the photo.

— stepping over blocks of cement, pieces of toys and furniture, avoiding iron rods and bits of broken glass windows — and I slightly panic wondering what the right words are to say to someone who lost her home, her belongings, her savings — maybe even her family.

But I do not get the chance to start talking, as she takes the lead in our conversation. First, she smiles at me — a big, broad, radiant smile — and then she offers to make me some coffee. Actually, she does not offer. She instructs me to receive coffee from her. What a beautiful instruction, what a generous invitation in the middle of this set-up.

She rummages for a hunk of brick upon which I could sit, then picks up a chipped cup missing its handle and a big, dark brown sock. She takes half of a handful of coffee from a plastic pot and pushes it inside the sock. While I am observing her movements, my mind gets curious wondering if the brown was the sock's original color. My guess is that it had been white in the past, so where has this brown come from? Coffee? Soil? Has it been used on a foot?

It is, after all, not even a week after a major earthquake. There is no way the sock now involved in this coffee preparation can possibly be clean. A light tension passes through my throat when thinking about it. But the smile and the shine of this woman brings my wandering mind back to the moment and my coffee that is almost ready.

She is now warming water on a little fire. After barely a minute or two, and before it boils, she pours the water in the sock over my piece of cup; and yes, I could see that the tinged sock makes for a convenient organic coffee filter.

I am thinking that a priority task of mine today is to assess with the team where we can install the water points, because the access to safe drinking water in the area is disrupted. Contaminated water needs to boil at least one minute, and the water has not even reached the boiling point.

Suddenly I understand that I am about to drink the first non-potable coffee of my life. But I do not care at all. I am not yet personally familiar with the physical consequences of drinking non-potable water, and, anyway, this moment is such an authentic, unique and warm one to enjoy — sock coffee or not.

This is a kind of moment you cannot organise, plan for, or purchase. In the middle of a disaster, in a setting that could be a horror movie, without knowing each other's names, without needing to know anything about each other at all, we are like two friends having coffee on a light and joyful day.

I am uplifted and fascinated by this woman's generosity and the connection that naturally happens between us. I am grateful to be in Colombia. I experience peace and bliss to be sipping coffee with her sitting on a brick, in the eerie calm after the quake, staring at a woman whose grand smile stares back at me.

She is not having coffee, I should add. She is simply enjoying her gift of coffee to me. We do not talk much, words are not necessary for the souls to be connected. We are sharing the suffering, the grace, the sisterhood and the love of the moment.

She says the temblor seemed it would never end. The trauma worsens with the aftershocks. Close to 30 she has counted. 30 mini-earthquakes, and you are so scared you will lose everything again, even what and who you do not have anymore. It feels that it will be your last moment on

Earth. It is like a nightmare from which you are not able to wake up.

Then she checks on how much I am liking my first Colombian coffee in Colombia. She apologises that she does not have the butter biscuits to enjoy with it. I tell her how enough everything is, how magic is the moment for me, and, in silence, our eyes turn towards the wall bearing the Phoenix message.

I finish my coffee, thank her with a *"miles de gracias"* and with subtle teary blurs in our eyes, we hug.

Time to go back to work.

***

15 years later, on another foggy day, surrounded by intact structures of concrete, steel and glass that stand fiercely and arrogantly high, I am sipping a nice almond-milk cappuccino. Colombian coffee? I am not sure.

I am in Bangkok reading an article on how diamonds are formed in the mantle of the Earth and delivered to the surface by deep-source volcanic eruptions, under scorching temperatures and tremendous pressure. I am impressed because I had no idea that diamonds would have this story.

What strikes me is that the more I learn of a diamond's journey, the more I see similarities between this precious stone and our personal and business lives. I have flashes of coaching sessions, public speaking training with people feeling and looking so disempowered and suddenly having this rush within, this sparkle in the eye and a shine coming up, an intense eruption coming from the core that is made of pain, of discomfort, of overwhelming heat but one that brings up the purest: the diamond.

When I revisit explosive and painful moments of my life, I can see the diamond that was expelled and brought to light.

I am thrilled by the powerful analogy of processes between nature and our lives: we go through the same to uncover the purest and the most solid parts of us.

I pick up my phone to check the etymology of the word "diamond." I love the etymology of words, because it takes us to the deeper meaning, the essential and spiritual one. "Diamond" is derived from the ancient Greek αδάμας (adámas). It means "unbreakable," "untamed."

A massive "of course" fills up my heart and my soul, the second part of my breakthrough is a vigorous reminder: it is out of these volcanic eruptions in our lives, these telluric movements provoked by the loss of a job, the bankruptcy of our business, the good-bye of the love of our life or a severe health issue, that the strength within shows up, pro-pelling us to overcome the hardship and bounce forward.

The image and the moment with my Colombian host-ess hits my memory. Her generosity, her ability to smile, this thought of preparing coffee for me when none of her basic needs were met. These were expressions of her inner diamond — the unbreakable and untamed essence that we hold within and that no circumstance or person can break or tame.

The earthquake broke her walls, but it could not break her foundations, her core.

The earthquake had destroyed her material resources but not the way she was nor her desire to be generous.

The earthquake left her alone and with nothing but her core, her raw essence — her inner diamond.

There was no social status, label, looks, property, title or position between us. She offered me a piece of her legacy, which came from who she truly is, no matter what, leaving her imprint on my life.

Thousands of people from more than 30 different nationalities have heard about her encounter with me, and so many report back how they cherish this story and how she has become part of them. Millions will read it and remember this woman whose name I never knew but who impacted so many lives by giving what she has: herself and her values.

We all have "us." We all hold an inner diamond that has showed up and emerged in our challenging times of life and has always been within us, even when or if we were blind to it.

It comes with creation; it is foundational. Like the natural diamond comes from the center of the earth, we have this *adamas* in our core and we consciously or unconsciously plant it in our projects and businesses.

Can you remember a period of your life when you felt an earthquake had devastated all areas of it, and yet you kept standing and are still here today? What about your business that you had to start from scratch again and is now not only on track but firing up?

We shine our diamond unknowingly, too, in the way we are, in the jobs we choose, in the way we do business, and in the products and services we sell. This is the first component of our legacy, each legacy being unique like every diamond is. We can start living our legacies without any specific strategy or budget, gradually increasing awareness and proactivity, converting over time into a focused and purpose-driven individual or corporate social responsibility.

We want to be conscious about this inner diamond so that we can tap into its resources, resilience and strength to build and live our legacies, without having to go through the earthquake, or at least learning from it, if we do.

After my breakthrough about nature and human diamonds, I got curious about the qualities of natural diamond, wondering if there were again any parallels with our human and business experiences that could be of service to our purpose.

The Gemological Institute of America (GIA) establishes the 4Cs of Diamond Quality as the universal method for assessing the quality of diamonds. They are: (1) Color, (2) Clarity, (3) Cut and (4) Carat Weight.

I like to use the same 4Cs to shape, revisit or structure our personal and corporate legacy and social responsibility strategies.

***

The first C is Color, referring to the lack of color, like a drop of pure water. This purity relates to our essence or the essence of what we do, without labels, or make-up, regardless of our belongings or capital, with no consideration of social status or size.

This is the starting quality of your organizational or project DNA and the first step of your legacy or social responsibility development.

- This is what you already do and radiate and what you can build upon.
- Think about your project, your organization or your business.

- List what you believe to be and experience as the essence of it. What does it give to people and to the world? Possible words that might come to mind are: authenticity, sustainability, efficiency, rapidness, commitment, care, healing, delivery, employment.
- Ask at least eight stakeholders (a mix of partners, clients and providers) to mention three qualities they associate your company with.
- Sit with your team and discuss the findings. Observe the commonalities and explore the differences.
- Keep three to five main descriptors. They are your first C: color or better said, the absence of color — your core values that are your root contribution, from where we will little by little build up, in the following chapters your purpose-driven social responsibility, by adding the Clarity, the Cut and the Carat.
- If you are doing it at individual level for your own individual social responsibility, your legacy, follow the same steps and ask friends and colleagues what qualities you radiate and embody.

Epilogue

Without getting into the scary details, I will share with you that later that night I ended up at a Colombia Red Cross field hospital with a rehydration drip for few hours. It had indeed been a non-potable coffee.

The optimist in me can say that it managed to strengthen my immune system considerably.

I also learnt a remedy from the doctor that day, which would later save me many many times: Coca Cola happens to be an excellent cleanser in this kind of situation and helps replenish fluids and glucose.

The human and spiritual aspects of me proclaim that this was one of the most transcendental moments of my life. Proof is that 20 years later, I am still shaken, moved and inspired, and I am sharing this story endlessly all over the world.

When you get up in the morning, before starting a meeting or inaugurating a conference, when presenting to potential investors or partners, when reflecting upon your strategy, when you feel lost or demotivated, remember the diamond that surged from the earthquake.

Notice the vibrant greens and reds, the extravagance and abundance that hide behind it. Smile and hold fiercely your color to ignite your motivation and that of your team. Inspire your marketing and broadcast your message to your clients, providers and to the world.

Do so, and you will see that you are already
living your legacy.

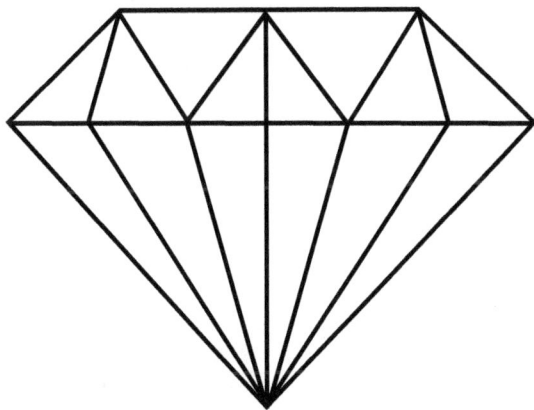

Chapter II

GUATEMALA

"In a gentle way you can shake the world."
Mahatma Gandhi

October 2004

Ride a donkey or walk? These are my transport options on a grey yet warm day in Guatemala.

I am thrilled to visit Guatemala for the first time. I am also nervous about what is to be seen, what will unfold. I like my job, especially its absence of routine. Disruptive and exciting events mean that each day holds a different gift, opportunity or challenge, like today's unusual decision to travel by foot or by four-legged beast.

Wouldn't it be exotic to arrive at work on a donkey? I think to myself.

But I choose to walk. The rocky, irregular path and the fact that I am in my first trimester of pregnancy are good enough reasons to trust my legs over my ability to wrangle a donkey.

Just last week, at my desk in Managua, Nicaragua, I received a phone call from an international humanitarian organisation working in Guatemala. They mentioned an area where malnutrition indicators had reached alarming levels, and they requested a joint field visit as soon as possible. I was soon on my way.

I am responsible for covering Latin America and the Caribbean as Rapid Response Coordinator of the European Union Humanitarian Aid Department. Whatever the crisis — natural disaster, socio-political crisis, displacement due to conflict — my job is to ensure an EU presence onsite quickly, to qualify the needs of affected populations, make strategic recommendations and protect as many lives and livelihoods as possible.

Three staff members of the organization pick me up at Guatemala City airport. We jump in their car to Huehuetenango department. After five hours of driving, we step out the car, because the road only continues straight, but our destination is toward the west. This is the point where cars cannot progress further, so donkeys are made available.

We start our walk through a monotone landscape of steep, grey stones and gravel. Few bushes give a hint of green color.

Who would want to live over here? I wonder.

No one, actually. Indigenous people have been pushed to relocate their homes and communities further and further, to the most inhospitable and barren areas of the country. Greedy landlords keep the fertile areas for themselves.

Upon arriving at the village, a group of children surrounds us. They are giggling and running after each other, and I cannot resist running around with them. The children are quite amused to have a stranger joining their fun.

Some have yellowish, sparse hair — one of the most common signs of malnutrition. A couple of them show distended bellies from water and fluid building up due to lack of nutrients. Others look quite strong.

Word must have passed through the village that strangers have arrived. Already a few people come to welcome us and enquire about the objective of our visit.

I leave the group of children a little short of breath, taking note of the vision of pinks, blues and reds worn by the women of the village. The colors lend much needed brightness and joy to the otherwise desolate environment.

There are no adult men, apart from a few elderly ones. Most younger men migrate to find labour work in sugarcane, banana or coffee plantations, having no choice but to work for perhaps the same families who evicted them forcibly from their lands.

The interpreter introduces us to our greeters in the local language. I can't understand what is being said, but they all point at the same wooden hut with a thatched roof. We wait for the village midwife to allow us to step inside the dwelling. She is the only one with enough authority to allow us to chat with a married woman when her husband is absent.

The lady of the house is pregnant too. Her belly is massive compared to her thin body. She gracefully invites us to come inside. In the center of the room, there is a *fogón*, a fire to cook and to heat the place. Cooking pots and a few vegetables are piled up in the kitchen area. The opposite side is reserved for the family bedding and clothing.

She takes us to her baby sleeping on a heap of colorful handwoven fabrics that have been organized to shape a little bassinet on top of a mud cabinet. The baby is so tiny, so cute, with dark eyes like his mum's. No hair. Guessing from his size, I think he is few weeks or months old. I ask the interpreter about his age, who asks the midwife, who in turn asks the mother. The reply comes as a shock: He is two years old. Two years old and as small as a newborn.

He is staring at me deeply without blinking. I feel as if I am alone in the world with him, locked in unbearable eye contact — unbearable because my soul is bleeding now at the sight of this baby dying of hunger right in front of me.

Hunger is not a problem of food. It is the most horrendous expression of inequality, injustice and negation of rights. I want to scream my anger and to curse the whole world for allowing this to happen.

I am carrying life in my womb for first time, experiencing the magic of the life to be born, and today I see a baby dying the most intolerable death. Reacting to this unacceptable contrast, my head spins, my chest pounds, my throat ties up in knots.

We are conversing with his mother, trying to understand their context, the food habits, the challenges. I cannot stop looking at him.

Shaky and wanting to collapse, I exit the hut and sit on a little stack of wood. I have to keep all these feelings for my inner world; it is only the beginning of the field visit. I want to steer my mind and heart to my objective here, so I can make the difference I want to make.

We proceed with the field visit, assessing the reality of other villages, families and health centers to get a more comprehensive understanding of the situation. Tomorrow will be dedicated to institutional meetings.

At the end of the day, back at the guesthouse, I throw myself on the bed. My bag still hanging from my shoulder, my blue and yellow-starred jacket on, I explode into tears. I am crying from my heart, my soul, my guts, my womb.

Hours pass before I stop crying. I see again his eyes in my mind, and I understand what they want to tell me: They are telling me he is hungry, and that it is my business.

It's not my business because I am a humanitarian worker but because I am human. We humans hold a social responsibility for what is happening or not happening, for what we choose to do or not do. We are brought to this world with talents, gifts and opportunities that are meant to be used. They are not meant only for us, our lives and our goals. They are meant to be given to our communities and to the world. They are meant to be shared.

When we mobilise ourselves and our skills to build something meaningful, we lighten our lives with increased purpose. Our drives are fueled with a sense of creating legacy. And we want more of it. It is through this process that we allow our inner diamonds to shine.

I start to think about my sense of purpose and legacy. Yes, I am doing daily humanitarian work. Yes, my dedication is one hundred percent. But am I using all of who I am? The answer is, no. There is more to explore beyond the usual business here.

The humanitarian organization medical team drove the toddler to the nearest hospital with a therapeutic feeding unit. But it was too late. The child was already in a coma — that's why his eyes kept staring at me. At a physical level, the staring was a manifestation of the coma, but I still cherish the experience that our souls communicated with our gazes.

I would have liked a happy ending, but he was gone.

And now, when I feel my heart constricting in pain, I remember that diamonds are made through high temperatures and pressure, and then I try as best I can to transform pain into drive and stress into the energy to move forward.

There is nothing we can do for this child but to hold him as a source of strength and inspiration: This is part of this young boy's legacy.

***

Eleven years later, I am invited to give the opening keynote at the "Universities Fighting World Hunger" event in Thailand, the first of its kind in the country. It is organized by students for students. I love that. I love working with youth.

The event is a full day of talks and sessions about hunger and its forms, the achievements, challenges and the way forward for a world free from hunger and malnutrition.

The audience consists of around 200 people, a mix of Dutch and Thai students. Ultra-blond hair alternates with jet black hair. The first row is filled by the professors and managers of the exchange program. The organising student team is roaming around industriously, wanting everything to be perfect. Everything is indeed perfectly set. The mics are working; the event starts on time; and video projectors are switched on.

They want me to motivate the students to commit to fighting hunger. They ask me to get the audience pumped up, so they thirst for the next presentations and take the full ownership of this initiative.

I tell the story of my Guatemala toddler under the title, "I am hungry, and it is your business."

Some weep during my speech.

A spiritual teacher once told me that tears are the expression of the soul being touched. When the soul is moved deeply, the next step is to identify how we can transform pain into meaning and legacy. This is done through taking one action. Any action. It can be small, or it can be big. It only needs to be an action.

Passivity ejects us from the change leader's seat, which may instigate a change that might not be the kind we want. But action gives us control over change. Action activates our self-esteem and confidence. It tells us that, yes, I am enough to make a difference.

Action helps us fine tune our strategy. Sometimes we get held back many years, or even a lifetime, wondering what our life purpose is. A simple action, even one based on intuition, will trace the beginning of our path and enable us to put words on our purpose so that we may live our legacies.

Standing before the rows of students, I make a call-to-action to ensure food for all. Not to cry collectively about malnutrition statistics, but to commit to recreating a world in which no one is hungry.

I ask the students what they want their roles to be. What legacies do they want to create? I invite them to live their legacies from that day forward.

I give each of them a piece of paper, a pen and an envelope. I ask them to write what they want to do — not what they can do, or what they think they will be able to do. The fullness of possibility, I explain, does not develop from defining what you can do but from defining what you want to do.

What do they want their dreams and visions in building a hunger-free world to be?

The students light up. They understand.

I see their excitement in their body language, their smiles and their sparkling eyes, the frenetic movement of hands writing.

As I look over the crowd of students, it's clear this is a magical moment of legacy in the making. I see their excitement in their body language, their smiles and their sparkling eyes, the frenetic movement of hands writing.

Pens are whispering bold dreams on paper.

We are all too often restricted to dream only what our parents, society and our own self-limiting minds have envisioned for us. This is why writing *what we want* is such a powerful exercise. It enables us to let go of years of focusing on what we can or cannot.

Writing physically and mentally frees the mind, too. What is on paper is not any longer trapped roaming around in our heads, where fear and doubt extinguish passionate dreams. Writing puts ideas in a physical place where we can gain new perspective. From this higher angle, we can assess our goals and desires through our eyes, separated from the internalized negativity that screens our thoughts and delays or prevents action.

***

Colombia showed me the inner diamond. Guatemala challenged me on the use I was making of my inner diamond: Was I keeping it in a safe? Was I holding myself back with self-limiting beliefs? Was I throwing it to a waste bin, or bringing it to its full shine?

When we start thinking about "how" before the "what," we get caught in our limiting beliefs. Feeling disempowered, we focus only on our "cannots." But when we envision what we want, we can draw up action plans that take us where we plan to reach. In this way, our dreams become our goals.

Imagine a physical diamond. What would you think of a person trashing it in front of you? What have you said about people keeping their gemstones at a bank safe and never wearing them?

We hold a duty to unpack our talents, to uncover our inner diamonds and to let them shine.

Unleash your inner diamond to the world no matter what. Don't chuck it in the dustbin or lock it in the safe. No one else can use it after you pass.

***

This duty gets embodied in the **second "c" of the diamond — clarity.**

The clarity of a diamond refers to its absence of blemishes. The exposure to tremendous heat and pressure deep in the earth can give diamonds blemishes or inclusions. Most diamonds have at least one or two, and the most valuable ones do not have any.

So, the second component of our inner diamond is what we are going to commit to without blemish. What are you clarifying and sticking to? What are you standing for without vacillation?

Look again at the color components of your inner diamond, the essential qualities that are the first step of your legacy or social responsibility development, as identified in Chapter One.

- How do you manifest these three to five values and qualities in your life, business or project? It can be in the way your customer service is designed, the mainstreaming themes of your project, your involvement in community service, or any area and activity that translates your values into practice. Write your response in the most detailed way possible.

- How would you like to manifest them? What are the areas of your life, business or project that you want these values to influence? We are defining what we want, so there is no limitation.
- What are the first three activities you are going to undertake and within which timeframe? The activities refer to actions to translate your values into the reality of your life, business or project. Specify in which areas and with whom.

Epilogue

Whether through spoken or written word, the story of the boy in Guatemala is hard to share. We are all scandalised by the idea of a child dying of hunger. It is depressing and makes us angry. And personally, I never want my audience to feel dragged down.

An important technique speakers use is lifting people's moods after an emotional story or statement. We do that through a joke or a light statement. You do not need to invent it, though. In every heavy story, there is lightness. In every dark tunnel, there is light. In every disaster, opportunity.

When I feel demotivated, or when I am wondering if I am living according to my purpose, questioning what I am really doing on Earth, I remember the young boy's eyes and I smile. He gets me back on track. He is also with me when I am in action, when I am into my purpose, and when I think I am saving the world.

His memory carries an empowering and invigorating stamp of legacy being a duty, a must, something to be done without any excuses.

The boy and his powerful message are forever tattooed in my heart and in my legacy.

So, what will you choose? To go by donkey or foot?

Whatever your choice is, when you step into your values without blemishes and translate them into actions, you are living your legacy.

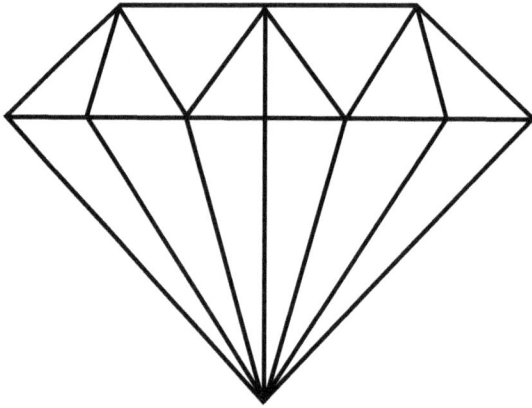

Chapter III

BOSNIA & HERZEGOVINA

"We are all meant to shine, as children do. And as we let our own light shine, we unconsciously give other people permission to do the same."
Marianne Williamson

December 1997

I am driving a little white van full of computers, car parts and office material. Departing from France, I am heading to Bosnia and Herzegovina for my first humanitarian mission. My co-pilot, an American, is also a new recruit.

We have a long journey ahead until we will reach Tuzla, the third-largest city of the country and my duty station for the coming months. During the 1300-kilometer drive, I'm wondering what will happen when we get there. A confluence of emotions — anticipation, trepidation, excitement — makes my palms bead with sweat, and yet I know already that no matter what happens on this mission, my first one ever, it will always hold a special place in my heart.

It is my first time driving through so many different landscapes. Twinkling Christmas lights and busy markets are here and there. The van is not that new. And the heating system? Well, it isn't exactly effective. But the radio is calling us to sing and forget about our freezing fingers and toes as we journey on.

We alternate driving, especially after nightfall. The ferry between Italy and Croatia lasts only few hours but gives us a welcome rest.

Upon arrival in Tuzla, three imposing power plant chimneys guard the town's entrance. Their smoke billows upward in hazy, puffy shapes then merges with the natural fog. (Tuzla is indeed always a bit foggy, and I enjoy the coziness it gives.) The way Tuzla looks is the way Tuzla is — authentic, without pretension.

In town, office buildings reminiscent of the Soviet era coexist with churches, mosques with slender minarets, and cafés with open terraces. Charming green, pink and yellow houses line the meandering streets.

The city is the headquarters of the American forces for the NATO-led multinational peace enforcement force. Their base is a town inside a town, complete with pavements and street names, famous brands of fast food, and even the only shop in the country selling authentic Levi's. Americans always impress me with their ability to create big things from scratch.

It is one of the most multicultural cities in the country and one of the few that was able to keep and reassemble much of its multi-ethnic population throughout and after the war. But Tuzla was not spared all atrocities.

It's been two years since the Dayton Peace agreements were signed in Paris. Humanitarian organisations are now slowly transitioning to income-generating projects to help war-affected people get back on track physically and psychologically.

Many people, especially those in the rural areas, still need basic food and hygiene packs to survive. Though the war might be over, wounds are gaping: Access and availability of food are issues. In many zones, landmines impede farming. Market chains are disrupted. Resources are scarce. These logistical challenges remind everyone that returning to normalcy may take time.

Luckily, it's easy to get working with the team. They had been longing for the new manager to arrive, and they know well the systems and procedures in each of their areas of work: logistics, administration and community work. I have three weeks to get acquainted with the work before I head to the field for my first food distribution.

On Christmas Eve, the team arrives at my rented apartment unannounced, bearing trays of homemade snacks and drinks. We barely know each other, and yet they cannot accept the idea of me being alone on the night before Christmas.

They hand me a gift wrapped in shiny paper. It's a CD of the artist Djordje Balasevic, famous for his poetic, anti-war songs. We pop the CD in the player, and I become an instant fan. I ask my new friends to help me write down the song lyrics, so I can join them for singing. It takes us at least an hour to transcribe and translate. We bond over this activity, which for me also serves as a crash course in the Serbo-Croatian language.

They tell me about their lives before and during the war and together we cry. We cry for their pain, losses and scars — in flesh and in soul. We cry also out of joy to be on this journey of recovery together.

At sunrise the day after next, we leave the warehouse with a five-ton truck filled with pallets of oil, pasta, tuna, salt, coffee, and other staples. The streets are snowy and winding. I trust the driver, but it is my first time in a truck. I feel like I am in a roller coaster, my belly turning somersaults from the ignorance of what is going to come next, as we traverse the slick, twisting road. Sometimes I close my eyes, so my mind does not exacerbate my fears.

We arrive after a couple of hours. The mayor is waiting for us in his office, with members of the council and other representatives from the community. It is so cold that we are all wearing layers of jumpers and big, woolen scarfs. There is a tiny heater, but I think it has more of a psychological effect than real, warming one.

A woman serves us steaming, Turkish coffee in tiny, carved cups. Work discussions won't start before the guests are properly welcomed, and these warm beverages help achieve just that. Simply seeing the coffee warms my body, and the smell of it makes me feel at home.

The spartan environment sets the stage for a mix of tension and excitement. These men are the age of my father, their weathered faces tell of the hardships they endured and the unspeakable things they saw or did when they lead army troops just a few months back.

Since the lady entered the office with the coffee-serving tray, all of us are silent, our eyes focusing on the movement of the cups being placed in front of each of us. Everyone is eager to feel heat on their lips and the sandy texture of coffee on their tongues.

The Mayor pushes towards me an opened pack of cigarettes. Unaware of local customs, I hesitate, confused by the contradiction between my belief that smoking a cigarette is inappropriate in a meeting with Government officials and the clear invitation to take one.

The mayor stares at me. I am the foreign guest, the one he wants to please and treat the most. I quickly look at my colleagues, trying to get an indication of what I should do.

As my eyes meet his, he says, "*Kava bez cigare kao dzamija bez munare.*"

Everyone jumps at translating for me. I don't react immediately because I am processing it: "A coffee without a cigarette is like a mosque without minaret."

I try to imagine a mosque without a minaret. Impossible. Likewise, it is impossible to refuse the cigarette.

This expression fascinates me, and I cannot stop smiling. Such a powerful image. Compelling. I like the sense of necessity and imperative of this expression. But I need to visualise things to anchor them and process the whole of them, so, with my eyes wider than the coffee cups we are being served, I ask them to write it down.

While one of the men gets a piece of paper and a pen, the Mayor pushes the pack towards me again. He pulls out the lighter. As a guest, it's time to take the cigarette so everyone can start enjoying their coffee. I pull out a slender cigarette, and the mayor lights it for me. There's a flash of heat and warmth in the cold and stark room, and something ignites in me as well.

***

22 years later, I remember perfectly the metaphor and I still write about it.

Can you imagine a mosque without a minaret? It would lose its essence. It would not be a mosque anymore.

What is so essential and compelling about the minaret?

Minaret comes from the Arabic word, *manara*, meaning lighthouse and watchtower. With light or without, it is always an elevated tower, something higher than the rest of the building.

From minarets, muezzins perch to make calls to prayer. A church's belfry serves a similar purpose — its bell's deep tone reminds people to head for service. The sound of the *adhan*, the call to prayer, is as typical of Cairo or Istanbul or Riyadh as the sound of bells in Rome.

Being a child of French Brittany, when I think of elevated towers, I also see the lighthouses of the Atlantic Ocean showing the path so our boats can safely reach the harbor.

Whether it is a chant, a ring or a light, the function — at physical and symbolic levels — is to guide us toward a path higher than where we are, a destination where we are safe and successful.

***

What would a mosque be without a minaret? Or a church without a bell tower? A coastline without a lighthouse?

Who am I, Amélie, without my elevated part? Without my purpose — my sense of legacy?

Who are we when we are not aiming high, when we are not into our inner diamond, when we stay at the ground floor in life, at work and in our community?

This question leads me to introduce the third "C" of your inner diamond: the cut.

We often think of a diamond's cut as a shape — round, heart, oval, marquise, or pear. But a diamond's cut grade is really about how well a diamond's facets interact with light. It is about symmetry, proportion and polish. The final beauty and value of the diamond lie in the cut.

The value of our inner diamond is in how we will put it to service, how we will allow its light to shine through the choices we make.

For the identification of the cut, there is a visualisation exercise that I invite you to take. Visualisation will help you connect with your more intuitive, soul-related and spiritual parts. You need to listen to that wisdom to reach the elevated towers of yourself, to cut your diamond into shapes that gives them maximum splendor, shine and radiance.

The mind is here for mapping, planning and implementation, and it usually rebels during this kind of exercise because it is scared to be overridden. The mind is fearful of the unknown.

In order to reassure your mind, I usually start this exercise, whether it is during individual coaching or teams' seminars, in a different space.

First, please move from your desk, change to a different meeting room or modify the chair and table arrangement.

Second, every important warm-up ritual involves breathing. Uncross your legs and arms, sit comfortably, close your eyes, inhale through the nose inflating your belly as if it were a balloon and exhale through the nose emptying your belly from all the air. Do this for six or seven cycles.

There are two options to undertake this exercise: visualisation through meditation or through a drawing.

- Choose to sit in your favorite meditative posture and corner or grab your personal notebook and some colored pencils.
- Create the intention of inner reflection on the cut you want to give to your diamond, the light you want to project as your legacy.
- Review mentally or reread what you came up with for the Color (*the three to five core qualities or yourself or*

your business) and the Clarity (*the current and upgraded translation of these values into your life or work*).

- Close your eyes, and visualise the mosque with its minaret, the lighthouse projecting light, the belfry ringing bells or whatever building you want to imagine with an elevated tower. If it does not match your belief system, it does not matter at all. We are not talking about religious or sailing affairs, we are simply using the symbols to define our legacies. Observe the building's shape, colors, energy.
- What is the call or the direction you would like this tower to give? To whom?
- Embody this tower, merge yourself with it and identify what is your role. If you are drawing, you can write on the drawing.
- After this visualisation exercise is finalised, write down all what you saw, experienced and felt. Don't censor yourself and include all the details. What maybe does not make sense today might make sense in five years. What you are not able to understand or to process may be essential in few days or few hours' time. Same for the drawing. Remember, it does not need to be shared (unless you wish). It is for your own process.
- If you are working on the exercise in a team, ensure you have created a confidential and sacred space of sharing and get people to share their meditation experience or drawing in groups.
- Wrap-up the process by writing in concise bullet points the path you want most to light up, the people you want to bring light to, and whatever other indications you have obtained from the exercise.

Epilogue

I tried many times to find Amira, Emir and the other colleagues again. We used to write to each other through post mail, but the change of physical addresses, the lack of constancy in writing, and our changing life circumstances made us lose contact. I feel sad about it, but I keep faith that I will get to hug them again in this life.

When I enjoy a cup of steaming coffee, it is not Turkish-style, and I don't light a cigarette anymore, but I like to remember that coffee does not come alone, and that everything given invites us to live for a higher purpose. We can choose how big we want the minaret, the lighthouse, the bell's toll to be.

When I feel nostalgic for my first mission, the one that will always hold a special place in my heart, I type "*Samo rata ne bude*" by Balasevic in YouTube. I forgot the lyrics I used to know by heart, but I still scream aloud with all my vocal cords and from my soul: *Samo rata ne bude. Just let there be no war. Just let there be no war. Just let there be no war.*

I remember the mothers, too, on the morning food distributions, who would ask me to sit next to them and tell me how their children have been killed. I cry remembering their pain. I cry also out of gratitude to have met and held hands with them, to have lived a piece of my life and my legacy with each of them.

I take my crying heart and eyes and promise I will use them to irrigate my legacy — not only wanting to impact others with my light but inspiring and mobilising everyone I can to let their diamonds shine.

Step up from the most elevated part of yourself
and shine up the world with your legacy!

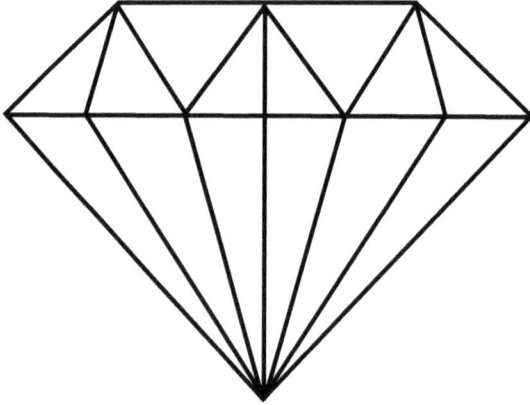

Chapter IV

CAMEROON

"It is not about resources; it is about resourcefulness."
Tony Robbins

27th November 2018

I receive an email from New York for an assignment to Cameroon to work on the elaboration of a disaster risk reduction project. In 28 years as an expatriate, the only French-speaking country I worked in is Haiti. Curious fact for someone whose mother tongue is French.

I jump out of joy to go back to work in Africa. Going to a country and a context new to me makes my adrenaline fly. The logistical race is launched, especially with organising care for my boys. They want to come with me. Africa calls them, being of service thrills them, and, to be honest, missing school is quite appealing too.

They daydream about going on a mission together, and I promise we will make it happen — soon. A family project outside our geographical borders. A project where we merge our love and legacies.

But for this trip, I must go alone. The human magic starts at the Brussels airport, where the waiting area for boarding is tiny and congested. There is only one coffee shop and a long line. It's the messy morning time. I feel sorry for the only counter attendant, who has no time to even breathe.

It's almost my turn. There is a woman with a toddler before me, just after an old man who is at the counter. The man is checking the different prices. He would like a soda, but his 2,50 EUR budget is not enough. The lady and her toddler smoothly move toward him. She asks if he would allow her to complement the required amount. He gracefully accepts, thanks her, and leaves with a bottle in hand and a smile from ear to ear.

This is the only moment the overwhelmed shop attendant stops and breathes. She tells the woman how much her gesture makes her day and inspires her. I feel the same way. This exchange adds to my excitement of what is to come. When the day starts so beautifully, it can only crescendo in beauty and meaning.

I arrive in Cameroon at night and I cannot get a very precise impression of what Yaoundé looks like. I will have to wait until tomorrow. But I am already enjoying the temperature — warm but not steamy.

I spend a few days in the bubbly capital of Yaoundé to meet main stakeholders and to wait for my paperwork, so I can travel to Far North. Noise and cars abound, just like in all bustling capitals, but it is tempered with the small-village feel of little street food stalls.

Among the 10 regions of Cameroon, Far North is the poorest one. It's a region disrupted by climate shocks, food crisis, Boko Haram's incursions, internal displacement and refugees. To get there, surface transport would take too long, and viable commercial aviation options are not available. It is therefore on a United Nations Humanitarian Air Service flight that I embark. A small, safe plane packed with staff from aid organizations.

We land in Maroua. Passengers clamber into vans and four-wheel drive vehicles. Mohammed, the office driver, picks me up and I jump inside the car — I really do have to jump because I am a short height, and the front passenger seat is so high.

Cameroon is often described as Africa in miniature, because of its diverse landscapes: white beaches, mountainous areas, tropical rainforests, savannah grasslands and desert. I enjoy watching the changing landscapes on both sides of the road as we travel. Mohammed and I have a lively conversation, too, giving me a direct and delectable glimpse into the local culture. In under 40 minutes, we discuss polygamy, divorce, love, diaspora, terrorism, weather, food — topics as diverse as the passing landscape.

The dry season is just starting, and the temperature is perfectly warm, with a little breeze that rustles the green and brown grasses of the savannah. There are small and dispersed trees and thorny shrubs, such as baobabs. It's the kind of environment where you'd expect a monkey or elephant to show up at anytime. I have my cellphone ready to take a picture to send to the boys. We only get to stop for a herd of cows to cross the road. I take my picture. Exotic it is and different for sure.

The cinematic landscape gives way to the hectic town of Maroua, with cars, motorbikes, shops and streams of people walking up and down. It's a sudden contrast. I cannot believe my eyes when I step into the Orange shop to buy a SIM card. It is so huge. Big speakers are outside, blasting loud party music and trumpeting the latest promotions.

The sound and hustle quiet down as we turn towards the UN office and guesthouse building. There's a restaurant, few residential houses, and Cameroon's army quarters and offices.

What grabs my attention is a thick, tarpaulin roof supported by four poles. The tarpaulin reads: *Photocopy – Printing*. There are no walls or curtains for this unusual shop; it is all open-air. There is quite a *va-et-vient* to access one of the two photocopy machines, right there in the middle of the sand. Who ever would have thought you could operate an outdoor copy shop in Cameroon, with just a tent, a few machines and a heap of sand? This is surely a sign of transforming the impossible into the possible. It makes me smile.

During the next days in the field, I visit rural communities, interact with volunteers in charge of early warning systems, hold discussions with mayors and commissioners, and listen to the leaders of the women's network.

I am where I feel alive. With people. No mask, no label, no cast. Souls discussing about human matters. Humans experiencing bold and authentic stories. I leave the first community with an enormous and tasty watermelon, a sweet gift by the President of the local Red Cross.

I encounter a three-year-old boy on my last day. When he sees me, he hides and screams from behind the shining red and orange *boubou* dress of his mum. In his eyes, I am a white foreigner, so his experience tells him I am most likely there to vaccinate him. It is only after careful observation of my movements and actions that he risks coming closer to me. I keep my hands high up, as if I was to be arrested, making sure he will not think I am trying to jab him with an inoculation. And on this final day of the field visit, my gift is a hardly-won kiss from this gorgeous little boy.

I have few hours left in Maroua to gather the maximum information to design and shape the most relevant project. I am with Charles, the office coordinator and my brainstorming partner, coming back from our last meeting. We decide to walk back as the distance is short.

When we reach the printing and photocopy shop, I stop. I am so intrigued and fascinated. I can now see it better than I did from the car. It is neat and well-organised. Where are the machines plugged in? I cannot find any trace of electric connection. I just see sand around. But the trays of the machines are going up and down, and printed paper is coming out.

One of my favorite quotes from American coach Tony Robbins comes to mind: "It is not about resources; it is about resourcefulness. That's it. This shop thrills me because it is a living expression of resourcefulness.

The shop owner did not have the means to rent or buy a shop, and yet still he runs his business. He is not focused on his limits but only on the world of creativity and possibilities.

I share my amazement with Charles and grab him to go in direction of the shop. We cross the street. I want to see it and take a picture. I want to share my excitement and inspiration with the world.

I go toward the person who seems to be the main man of the shop. I tell him how much he embodies resourcefulness to me. I add that I want to share his story with the whole world. His shop can be an inspiration for those in doubt, for those stuck and thwarted by their perceived limitations.

I ask permission to take a photo. I am speaking at full speed, and I guess with my cheeks a bit red, too. I am feeling a little silly, I guess because I fear rejection. How will I feel, in front of all these men, if he says no?

He looks at me, sort of gauging how sincere I am and probably very surprised by my request. Maybe he thinks I am a little crazy. Maybe he is touched. Who knows? I have learnt to never assume what people think.

He says yes to the picture.

***

I now live in Europe, after 22 years of absence. I am enjoying living back in a state with rule of law, social security and a developed support system. Every day, I feel grateful for this abundance. But every coin has two sides.

I observe how people seem unaware of the quality and quantity of resources available. I observe how many people tend to look at the availability of external resources or its unavailability, rather than at their inner resourcefulness.

This is the drawback of a system where the State is given such a prominent foster role. We forget we are here first, wholesome and resourceful. We hand over our power and responsibility to an institution. The challenge lies in finding the balance between a supportive government, which cares for the most vulnerable, while still offering opportunities and a space where we rely first on ourselves, where we trust our abilities, and where the most resourceful can create a ripple effect that leads to more opportunities for others.

This is an issue I am called to explore.

The Dalai Lama likes to say world peace depends on inner peace. He says global issues cannot be solved without first attending our own emotional lives.

This approach applies to resources and resourcefulness.

Is it sustainable to count on resources and never take into account our resourcefulness? When we are into our resourcefulness, we are able to create. And we are also able to *attract* resources.

Resources enable you to walk your way, but resourcefulness drives you all along. Resources can terminate; resourcefulness has no expiry date. Resources are external, even when they belong to you. Resourcefulness is you.

What does it mean to be resourceful? It means thinking out-of-the-box, envisioning all the possible ways to achieve what we desire. It is a very precious skill to be able to intelligently and creatively use and attract resources.

Resourcefulness has three features:

- The first component is the intuition, the call, or the gut feeling that gives ideas, shows the direction to take, and keeps our spirits high. It is the sense of possibilities.
- The second is the courage, to dare to move forward, to take a leap of faith and assume full responsibility for one's life.
- The third is the acknowledgment that we have skills, intelligence and knowledge – and the ability to gain new knowledge when needed.

Looking with perspective on your most recent ventures, have you listened to your inner calls? Have you been courageous and daring? Were you confident enough in trusting your common sense and intelligence? How much did you honor your resourcefulness?

Be aware of your tendencies and take the time to evaluate what is at stake and how you can be at your maximum resourcefulness. Check on your knowledge and skills, reconnect with past situations that you successfully dealt with, celebrate your abilities, and decide on how to apply those to the current situation.

***

Resources and resourcefulness make a beautiful pair. As an entrepreneur, a homemaker or a project builder, you ideally want to have the pair.

And this pair forms the fourth and last "C" of the inner diamond: the Carat.

Carat is the weight. It measures the diamond's apparent size.

Our weight is how we are going to be able to maximise our Color, Clarity and Cut to unleash all the shine of our diamonds.

The weight depends on our resourcefulness in its double dimension:

1. The inner drive to overcome limitations and get things done with limited or no resources
2. The ability to attract and manage resources.

We all have different levels of resourcefulness, both innate and due to circumstances. It can be developed and enhanced. It needs to be nurtured under all circumstances. Indeed, someone can be very resourceful but when they are burnt out or unbalanced, they won't be able to connect to it.

The "weight" takes us to this sense of gravity and alignment with the core. At our best, we are centered, balanced, and strong.

Here are a few steps to help you "gain weight" in purpose and legacy.

Legacy weight gain program – individually or in team – for whatever types of projects, businesses or activities.

- Take your findings for color (three to five core values), clarity (activities that translate your values into action) and cut (your bigger vision).
- Look at the three features of resourcefulness (intuition, courage, acknowledgment) and identify which ones are strong or weak. As a business, you can explore this based on past decisions or new ventures.

Look at the resources you have. If there are zero other resources, connect to your resourcefulness.

- Be grateful for the resource(s) you have already.
- List the resources you need for the implementation of your business plan, new project or goal.
- Check what you really need, and remember that perfectionism is a killer.
- How can you obtain the required resources? Brainstorm on those that seem impossible and step into intuition, inner knowledge or courage.

Epilogue

The name of the owner of the printing and photocopy shop was Adam. After I took his clip, he made a sign that he wanted to talk to me. I was really excited. Until now, he had not shown huge interest in speaking – actually no real interest at all.

"Don't you have anything to print out from your iPhone?" he asked.

I felt so embarrassed, but my reply was no. I wished I had something.

After the first reaction of embarrassment, I was again full of so much admiration. Until the last moment, he did not lose the sense of business and resourcefulness.

Never give up, be strong, bring your weight and don't give up until you get there — that was clearly his message to me and to you today.

The days when you feel down, when you feel you cannot, when you are not being helped, remember Adam, the four poles and the tarpaulin.

Unleash the Adam in you, inspire others
to do the same and live your legacy!

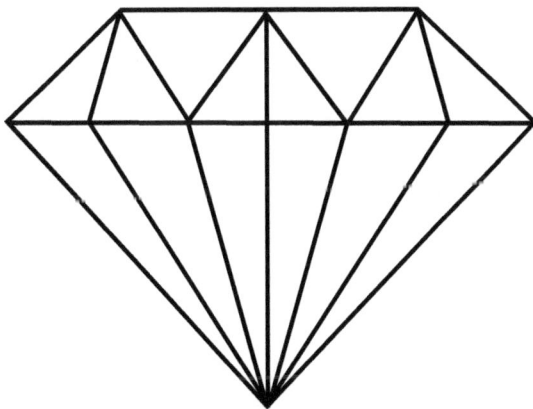

Chapter V

YOUR INNER DIAMOND: THE HEART OF YOUR LEGACY

"Here is the secret sauce: the more you invest in your mission, the more profits your business will produce."
Daniel Gilbert.

Colombia, Guatemala, Bosnia and Cameroon have opened us up to The Four C's – Color, Clarity, Cut and Carat. Together, they describe the characteristics of your inner diamond., the personal or the corporate one.

Your inner diamond holds your legacy, which you consciously or unconsciously live or which may be dormant at this time in your life.

THE 4CS
OF YOUR INNER DIAMOND
The Heart of Legacy

COLOR
= Who we are
As a person or as a company

CLARITY
= What we already do
At work, at home and in different departments

CUT
= Where we want to go
The big vision

CARAT
= How we go
Our inner and outer resources

Color is your essence, the core of who you are. It is the "being" part of your legacy. By being or becoming who you chose to be, you already make available your imprint on people's lives, your community and the world. The Colombian woman had lost everything and yet she marked her imprint on my life and now on yours.

Clarity is how you currently manifest your essence. It is what you already do, where you are right now in terms of our legacy. The Guatemalan baby compels you to translate our talents into actions ASAP.

Cut is your vision, the big dream. It is where you want to head - the next step or ultimate goal of your legacy. The Bosnian Mayor invites you to elevate our spirits and contribution to the world.

Carat is your resourcefulness, including your ability to attract resources, and form the available vehicles to reach destination. Adam from Cameroon confirms that there are always resources at your disposal.

In life or business, this diamond is the heart of your legacy. After you acknowledge and capture your legacy, all you must do is speak and live it, as we are going to explore in chapters six and seven.

Remember that your diamond is unbreakable, it will always be there, even when your business or personal life goes through ups and downs, even when you feel disconnected from it.

Your legacy may grow in other directions, too, like it did for me when I left my day job in international organisations to enter entrepreneurship. It was not an easy nor straightforward task to re-qualify my mission and my legacy on a totally different path. But I was the journey I had to walk. Each of us must walk our oaths and at the same time be prepared for change.

Let us put words on your inner diamond, so you can be more strategic about your social responsibility or contribution strategy.

Personal Inner Diamond

If you are to do the proposed exercises for yourself, you can complete them on your own. However, I suggest having a pair or a group of friends. Sharing in a group brings a higher dimension of support, accountability and commitment to the final outcomes.

Solopreneurs

Are you a solopreneur? Then proceed as mentioned above for personal inner diamond – either on your own, or, ideally with a group of other solopreneurs.

SMEs (Small and Medium Enterprises)

If we are talking about shaping the legacy of a company with multiple staff members, the exercise should definitely be a team effort. The dynamics will vary according to the size of the company. For companies with more than eight employees, select a facilitator to guide the exercises.

Large Companies and Organisations

I recommend that large companies split the employees into groups, ensuring that various departments are represented in each group. This exercise is a powerful opportunity to unite or re-unite the different teams around the core values and mission statement of the company.

Each staff member can also do the same exercise for themselves and on their own, to see how their work in the company adds to their legacies.

Color

- A few weeks before the exercise contact at least eight stakeholders (a mix of partners, clients and providers) and ask them which three qualities they associate with your company.
- List what you believe and experience as the essence of your business. What does it give to people and to the world? Possible words are authenticity, sustainability, efficiency, rapidness, commitment, care, healing, delivery and employment.
- Sit with your team to discuss the findings. Observe the commonalities and explore the differences. If you are a solopreneur but completing the work in a group, discuss the findings but do not compare, as you each operate separate businesses.
- Keep and write down three to five main qualities. They are your first C: color or better said, the absence of color. They comprise your core values that are your root contribution. These main qualities are from

where we will build up, little by little, in the following chapters to clarify your purpose-driven social responsibility, when we add in the rest of the four C's.

Clarity

- How do you manifest these three to five values and qualities in your life, business or project? Write your response in the most detailed way possible. It can be in the way your customer service is designed, the mainstreaming themes of your project, your involvement in community service, or any area and activity that translates your values into practice.
- How would you like to manifest them? What are the areas of your life, business or project that you want these values to influence? We are defining what we want, so there are no limits.
- What are the three first activities you are going to undertake and within which timeframe? The activities refer to actions to translate your values into the reality of your life, business or project. Specify in which areas and with whom.

Cut

- Choose if you are going to do the exercise through writing the meditative visualization or drawing and organise the appropriate set-up.
- If you are doing it in a team, you must first ensure a confidential and sacred space for participants so that

they feel safe and comfortable sharing their experience.

- The facilitator invites the participants to close their eyes and guide them with the following instructions:
- Create the intention of inner reflection on the cut you want to give to your diamond, the light you want to project as your legacy.
- Close your eyes, and visualise the mosque with its minaret, the lighthouse projecting light, the belfry ringing bells or a different building with an elevated tower. Just choose the building that naturally comes. If it does not match your belief system, it does not matter at all; we are not talking about religious or sailing affairs, we are simply using the symbols to define our legacy. Then, observe its shape, colors and energy.
- What is the call or the direction you would like this tower to give? To whom?
- Embody this tower, merge yourself with it and identify what is your role. If you are drawing, you can write on the drawing.
- After the visualisation exercise is finalised, write down all what you saw, all you experienced and felt. Don't censor yourself and include all the details. What maybe does not make sense today will make sense in five years. What you are not able to understand or to process may be essential in few days or few hours' time. The same applies for the drawing.
- Wrap-up the process by writing in concise bullet points about the path you want most to light up, the people you want to bring light to, and whatever indication you have obtained from the exercise. For the

group, the facilitator will wrap up and get the group agree on the final statement.

Carat

- Study the three features of resourcefulness: intuition, courage, and acknowledgment, and identify which ones are strong or weak for you. As a business, you can explore this based on past decisions or new ventures. For this exercise only, it is interesting to form department-based groups to learn from the existing pool of resources within the team.
- Look at the resources you have.
- Be grateful for the resource(s) you have already.
- List the resources you need for the implementation of your business plan, new project or goal.
- Check what you really need and refine your list of resources.
- How can you obtain the required resources? Brainstorm on those that seem impossible and use intuition, inner knowledge or courage, whatever it takes to come up with creative solutions.

Now that you have the 4 Cs of Your Inner Diamond, you are fit to Speak and Live Your Legacy at the next level, whether it is for your personal journey, the mission of your company, or your social responsibility strategy.

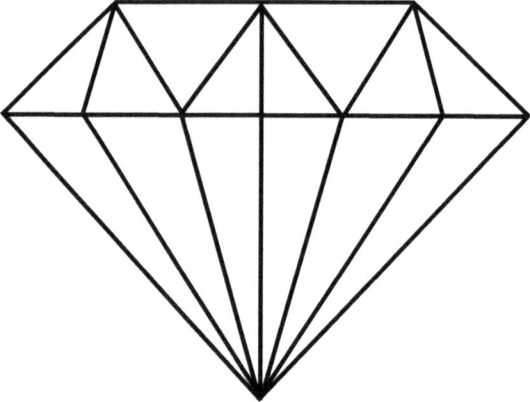

Chapter VI

AFGHANISTAN

"I alone cannot change the world, but I can cast a stone cross waters to create many ripples."
Mother Teresa

27th October 2017

I am landing in Afghanistan, the second country on my list of must-visit countries. It is a dream becoming a reality.

I am wearing a long black and white Indian dress, and, with a *dupatta* scarf on my head, I feel no different, really, from the other passengers. There are so many other blue eyes, though Afghan ones.

I am standing in line to deboard the plane. A young, dark-haired and green-eyed man is conversing with the air hostess. But he is staring at me. When I arrive at his level, he insists on carrying my hand luggage down the stairs.

Am I that old to be pampered by the younger ones? I think to myself. Or is it that he just wants me to feel welcome? Could it be I look absolutely irresistible?

It surprises me that men and women can connect and relate to each other so naturally and spontaneously. I am touched by the sweetness of the gesture. The queen in me enjoys being pampered by such a handsome man.

I am astonished by the beauty of the women and the men, not to speak of the children. Dark hair, large eyes with different shades of brown, blue or green. Harmonious facial features.

On the tarmac, I exchange a few words with the Afghan gentleman. Names, origin, reason for being here in Afghanistan. I elude answering the question of where I am staying, for security reasons. He asks for my Facebook details so we can connect. I give them.

In countries at war, intelligence services from whatever sides often connect with you under unsuspected covers. My humanitarian times taught me that transparence is the best armor. When people see what you do and why, there is no scope for imagination and assumption. You can then do your work. You have higher chances of coming back home alive.

I am torn between the excitement of showing off to my girlfriends that a gorgeous Afghan man was taking care of me even before I set foot on Afghan soil and the disappointment that his interest might only be to track who I am and what I am doing in Afghanistan.

I am in Mazar-e-Sharif, the fourth largest town of the country, up there in the North. It's the first time I see that many stalls of almonds, prunes, dates, all kind of nuts – everywhere in an extravagant abundance. Taxis, cars and bicycles coexist in a delicious noisy chaos. The day of bazar, the number of men, women of children in the streets, running up and down, passing from one stall to another is overwhelming.

Waiting for the luggage, I see a couple of ladies from the same family wearing the light blue burka with mesh screen I have seen so many times on TV. The rest of the ladies are dressed similarly to me. Accompanied by husbands and children, they seem to be coming home.

My colleagues for this assignment are five professional trainers from Delhi, who present on topics of leadership and talent development. We count 11 suitcases, not only because of carrying winter clothes but also the training materials. Our assignment is a one-week leadership training to high-level civil servants of Afghan government — a total of sixty women.

Our home for this week is a guesthouse that is bunkered for security reasons. It is late at night. Light is scarce in the streets and I can't see much. I am wondering if the famous blue mosque is nearby. It is said to be one of the most beautiful buildings in Afghanistan.

Upon arrival, we are assigned the rooms. I crash fast, enveloped in two thick, orange-and-yellow blankets with a floral print. The silence is disrupted by deep regular snoring sounds. Thank God, the sound is far enough so as not to disrupt my sleep.

I am an early bird. When I wake up, from my window I can see the rooftops of the neighborhood and an amazing pastel yellow color invading the sky — as if it was inundated with gold. I enjoy the miracle of nature few minutes. My training colleagues are not yet out of their rooms, so I make a guess on where to head. I am the first one at breakfast.

The table is huge with seats for 40 people. I mistakenly sit in the area for participants. But there are never truly wrong moves in life. By the time I sit and look around, some five to six women arrive for the breakfast feast.

I start a lively conversation with my neighbors. They all work in Kabul, where the government is based, but many have families in Mazar. Kabul is a tough place to be, with almost daily attacks and bombs. When they go out to work, they do not know if they will make it back home in the evening.

The guest house staff is placing round, honey-colored breads in front of us. Clearly, they are home-made. I am happy I do not facilitate today. When I do, I fast to keep my level of energy high. But today I can eat, so I indulge in this delicious bread. I am French, so the taste for bread is part of our genes, I believe. These breads are outstanding, beyond expectations.

The training days are intensive and intense. Split into two groups, we cover all aspects of leadership: emotional management, public speaking, team work, talent development, project strategy, motivation and self-confidence. The participants actively share. They also ask many questions and make many demands. It seems each moment is outside their comfort zones, but they want to learn and grab every bit of this opportunity for growth.

The day ends with a gathering outside the rooms. We remove our shoes and sit on large wooden bunks with colorful cushions. It is cold, but our pashmina shawls help us enjoy the warmth of the moment. We drink tea, eat nuts and pomegranate and then move on to dinner, without shifting position.

We discuss food, relationships, beauty tips, politics, war, religion — we re-invent the world.

After dinner, we walk up and down behind the high walls with barbed fences. We make many return trips, because there are barely 20 meters between walls. As we walk, we link arms, and they tell me their stories: what life was like before the Talibans. What it was when they arrived. What it is now today. We squeeze each other's hands as a sign of togetherness. We hug when the tears flow. We laugh out of gratitude to know each other.

I look at the guards with their Kalashnikovs. I am always so grateful for people exposing their lives for protecting mine and others'. I ask someone to translate for me. I want to say thank you. The guards smile back at me and acknowledge by nodding.

The staff of the guesthouse are very caring, constantly checking if anything is required. The homemade, organic food they prepare is a celebration of abundance, deliciousness. They are worried that my vegetarian diet might limit what they can treat me with.

There are few men aside the guards and hosts – two are from the organising UN Women agency and three interpreters. They join us in the discussions. It feels surprising to have this closeness and harmony with men in such a context. It gives me hope. It shows me that the worst systems cannot break us, that prejudices never represent real life.

One of the guesthouse staff shows me a video of his nephew dancing a traditional Afghan dance. Women cannot dance in presence of men, but men can. We are seven of us, deciding simultaneously that we would like him to dance for us. A woman chooses the music. He feels shy, but we insist. We verbally drag one of the other men to join him. We clap, we encourage loudly, we holler in a beautiful moment of laughter and connection.

When it is time to head to bed, there is always one of them asking me to wait for a few minutes. She then reappears with a jewel, a scarf, sweets or nuts. A gift for me, to bring back home, a gift to experience Afghanistan differently than how the country is portrayed on TV, a gift because they love to give. They live in a constant state of war and they know, better than anyone, the importance and relevance of all these moments of life.

In a war context, there is no time to lose. Relationships are immediate, raw and real. They are profound and authentic.

Every minute of my stay in Mazar-i-Sharif offers me a gift and a lesson.

One of my favorite sessions is the elevator pitch. It gives you 60 seconds, about the length of an elevator ride, to present yourself. An elevator pitch is an empowering moment to dare being and sharing who you are. In all our societies, the first seconds you speak make a huge difference on the connection you create, the impression people make on you and on your ability to be heard.

They share how important it is for them, as women, as senior leaders at the government or parliament. They crave to speak, rise and to contribute to creating peace and stability in their country. They are often not listened to because they are women, but they want to be heard. They want to know all the techniques to help them project their voices and broadcast their messages.

I want everyone to practice the 60-second presentation and receive personalised feedback. I am almost about to achieve my objective, but one of the participants says she does not want to stand and speak. I ask a couple of times more, gently, without pressure, to re-open the opportunity. Her no seems final.

The session is finishing. We clap for the last presenter, and I am ready to conclude and close when the lady who refused to speak asks to be given her turn.

I am surprised. The time is up, but everyone is eager to listen to the reticent participant to present herself and her mission in 60 seconds. She is impressive to look at. I gauge her size to be more than six feet tall. She has a determined and authoritative presence, and she starts her speech looking right at me. I can tell she is talking to me, but I am waiting for the interpretation to reach my ears.

She is saying she feels tired, exhausted, with a migraine and low on energy — not an ideal state for giving a speech, to be sure. I am feeling a little tense of what she might say – what urges her to stand and to speak? I am wondering if she got upset with something and that perhaps I am going to have to handle this at the end of a very powerful workshop. I fear all the amazing energy may get shattered.

She says she recognizes my efforts, energy and passion for getting all participants present themselves with impact, giving all what I have and know to make it happen. She felt guilty about not grabbing the opportunity herself, despite all my enthusiasm and participatory spirit. She decides she has no right to keep sitting and not giving her all, too.

I am blown away, moved almost to tears by her comment. My soul pulsates with excitement. I never heard that in any workshop before. Yes, I heard beautifully touching expressions of gratitude but never an expression of the compelling nature of daring to speak your legacy.

She does not feel like speaking, but she is going to speak and say what needs to be said in this moment. She follows this inner instinct, the inner "must."

She introduces herself, her job and her love for her country. She seduces the audience with her authenticity, her courage and the leadership she models. Everyone breaks into applause, lifted by her spirit.

***

When someone dares, it automatically uplifts and inspire others.

How many times have you turned off the opportunity to show up or to share your message? There was always the perfect excuse — feeling unworthy or illegitimate, not having had time to prepare, lack of self-confidence, fear of rejection. The list is endless when it comes to what we let get in the way of standing and speaking, of sharing our messages and letting our inner diamonds shine.

"I want to speak in public but first I need to gain self-confidence." Is this something you have said or felt? There are words I hear often in my workshops. I give the same response every time it comes up: Confidence comes with speaking. Confidence is not key to convince an audience, authenticity is. Your color, your clarity, your cut and your carat. Your inner diamond, the heart of your legacy, is what the world craves hearing.

The Afghan lady did not gain a round of applause due to demonstrating public speaking techniques. She gained it because she had showed her real self.

So many people do not dare speaking because their English is not fluent. People are not listening to you to get an English language class, but to hear you.

It is not about your language, it is about your message

How do you speak your legacy and share your message, even if it is not perfectly refined or defined?

The first technique I would like to share with you is: *Fake 'til you make it.* Is that contradictory to the message of authenticity? Not at all, this invitation is not about faking the message, but faking confidence through body language. When you fake confidence, you cheat your mind first and it makes easier to step authentically into confidence.

The second technique I want to share with you is the secret of public speaking: *Love yourself*. I can imagine your reaction of surprise and maybe disbelief toward this affirmation. It took me few years of speaking to find out that the secret of public speaking, more than any technique, is really about oneself – knowing, trusting and loving who you are.

When we stand to speak, our first reaction is wanting to be loved. We expose ourselves physically, emotionally and even spiritually – it comes with a lot of vulnerability. We have been educated to please others: parents, teachers, society, spouse etc., so each time we expose ourselves, we believe we have to fit others' expectations.

When you had this objective in any kind of relationships — the objective of pleasing — have you ever succeeded? On the contrary, you may have lost your partner or the colleague and even yourself.

Speaking is about sharing a message — not about pleasing anyone. You can actually displease people and yet succeed on your goal of sharing a message. Imagine you are the director of human resources and you have to fire 30 percent of the staff. You organize a team meeting and it is very unlikely they feel love and tenderness for you in the moment. But still, your message can be clear and impactful.

When you focus on winning the love of your audience, you are into your personal agenda and not into your gift to your audience. That gets heard and felt by your listeners. There is a disconnection. And what a stress it is to carry the intention to be loved by one person or a crowd! This is one of the main reasons of our fear of public speaking: the fear of not being loved. Your focus needs to shift from seeking acceptance to your gift to the public, which is your message.

Speak Your Legacy with Self-confidence

You can fake your self-confidence until it is endorsed and comes naturally. Here is how:

Firstly, smile before, during and after the speech. The serotonin release provoked by the smile serves as a mood lifter: you will feel more confident and look more confident. Smiling people do look authentic and at ease.

Second, learn a useful tip for stress management by rolling your shoulders back. Practice in front of mirror a comfortable shoulders posture. Observe what happens when you roll your shoulders back: increased confidence, elongated spine, an opened throat. You feel good and you look taller. You will have increased charisma to help you stay on track to speak and live your legacy.

Third, remember to focus on your message. Beforehand writing your speech or presentation, it is essential you define the key messages of your talk. You should know well the points you want people to go back home with, and it is recommended a maximum of three for people to remember with ease. Once you have clarified your message, you start writing your text or preparing your presentation slides. When you are about to start speaking, your stomach may be overwhelmed by butterflies. If this happens, breathe and say to yourself, "It is not about me, but it is about them; let me give them my message."

Epilogue

I am connected on Facebook with my Afghan gentleman and we chat from time to time. When he reads this story, he probably will laugh out loud. I do not think he is actually from the Secret Services. I never asked why he connected with me. A little of mystery in life is always an enchanting spice.

Whatever your life pains are, when the little voices inside your mind tempt you to stay within your comfort zone, remember the Afghan lady.

Jump out of your seat, stand with a smile and open shoulders. Share your message and speak your legacy. And don't delay. You want to live your legacy now.

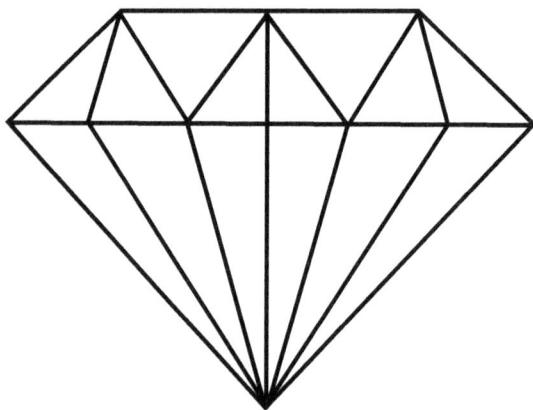

Chapter VII

NORTH KOREA

*"Out beyond ideas of wrongdoing and right doing
there is a field. I'll meet you there."*
Rumi

July 2013

His hypnotizing eyes are as dark as his jet-black hair. Looking barely 25 years old, he is a tall, handsome solider, dressed in a crisp brown uniform, with a big, red star emblazoned on his cap. He smiles at me — a warm and wide smile — welcoming me to the airport in Pyongyang.

The soldier cannot speak English, so it is with body language that he invites me to move to the right side of the security room. The screening machines, desks, and all the decor, in fact, feel as if they are from another era. It reminds me of a movie set during the Cold War — the kind full of intrigue, espionage, and cinematic tension between good and evil.

I am ecstatic to set foot in North Korea, which its citizens and government call the Democratic People's Republic of Korea, or DPRK. Only one staff member from our Bangkok-based regional office has ever been here before, and I know my colleagues would like to be in my shoes right now. It is always exciting to go those special places where not many are granted access. All of last week, since getting my visa, I had been bragging in the office like a frat boy.

And now, here I am. In North Korea, in flesh and in soul, observing with my own eyes bits of a country that is usually so negatively depicted. Much of the news focuses on the politics and system as if there were no nation, people or humanity. The "hermit Kingdom," they call it, as if its exile from the fraternity of nations is entirely self-imposed. But behind all shallow clichés and stereotypes, reality always lurks. And so, I want to know: How are the people of the country? What do they look like? What are their idiosyncrasies? What are their habits, their stresses, their dreams?

Immigration desks typically produce anxiety, especially in countries where the rules and laws are quite different. I am jittery from a mix of stress and excitement, like I feel after overindulging caffeine. Are they going to take my cell phone and keep it locked until my return? Am I carrying something that I should not have? Have I forgotten to bring some document that is absolutely necessary to get into the country?

"Do you have a photo camera?" the young immigration officer asks. I quickly pull my phone out of my bag and hand it to him. "Does it have GPS?"

One thing I am not is a tech geek. So, feeling surprised to hear this kind of phone could even have GPS, I flatly say, "No, it does not have GPS." Such technology, along with things like Western movies, are strictly forbidden in the North, whose citizens' lives are strictly controlled.

He passes my phone under a screening machine. After turning the device around in his hand, he comes up to me. He shows me that "G-P-S" is written, in big, fat letters, right across my phone. I'm horrified. I can feel my face goes pale. I think the worst: He will think I've lied! But he says it's okay, and he's still smiling. Perhaps he guesses that I had no idea there was GPS technology on my phone — that maybe I have no clue what GPS even is, let alone how to use it.

Every visitor in North Korea must be accompanied by a person who ensures the tourist knows and follows the rules . So, just as expected, after collecting my suitcase, my guide finds me and introduces himself. He asks about me, my family status and my age. He then says I am not to leave the hotel under any circumstances without first informing him. My guide will be staying in the same hotel, and if I want to go anywhere then he must come along.

He is a bit gruff but sweet at the same time. He lists what I am going to see: the monument to the Workers Party founding, the Taekwondo palace, the stamp museum, the arch of triumph, the Tower of the Juche Idea. The tower, the tallest monument in the nation, honors a North Korean ideology established by the nation's late founder, Kim Il Sung, grandfather of current leader Kim Jong Un. It stipulates that human beings are masters of their destiny – and masters of the revolution. It advocates self-reliance to achieve true socialism.

As my guide chatters on, I drink in every detail of my new environment. Pyongyang looks like a city where you'd want to live if you have children. There are many bicycles and few cars. Houses are painted pastel colors — blue, green, yellow, pink. The avenues are broad and generous. There are many pleasant, verdant parks. All around are huge monuments, sculptures and paintings dedicated to the celebration of the party and its leaders.

In a number of areas in town, people are rehearsing for the Victorious Day in July. My guide tells me they have been practicing every day after work. The residential buildings are very simple, and the citizens take good care of them. People clean, tidy things, and plant little plants here and there. Overall? It appears nice.

We take the metro en route to the contingency planning workshop. Again, it's like a movie set. The train and its tracks are deep underground — according to my guide, the Pyongyang metro is the deepest in the world. It is an old system but perfectly maintained. Sumptuous crystal chandeliers dangle from the ceiling. Colorful marble mosaics represent scenes of their "eternal president," the man credited with liberating them from the Japanese. Local newspapers are available for everyone's perusal, presented under glass stands.

The people I encounter are friendly. They smile, but not too eagerly. They seem curious, too, but they are discreet and don't ask me any questions. The exception is my inquisitive guide, who wants to know every detail about me, but I guess this is part of his job.

This training event with the international community is a rare occurrence in North Korea. The government requested the United Nations' support — likely the fruit of many years of humanitarian diplomacy and a call for a better response to the droughts and floods that regularly impact the country. The power of disaster preparedness is that it is not a political topic. It creates a space where people who may be suspicious of each other can sit, discuss and work together. This one of the reasons why this topic is my passion: it saves lives, it empowers people and governments and we can meet "Out beyond ideas of wrongdoing and right doing" as Rumi says.

The room setup is no different from any other workshop I have attended – round tables, a projector and a coffee break outside. People present, and those in the audience ask questions. At each table, there is a Korean participant who speaks English and ensures the translation. I am the only foreigner at my table. The five other people are technical staff, engineers or programme coordinators from different ministries.

Our group is efficient. We finish our group work earlier than the others and are waiting for the others to complete their work. No one is talking after this long day of presenting, brainstorming and discussing.

I am sitting across from an engineer from the Ministry of Transport. He squirms a bit and looks over in my direction. He looks to be slightly older than me. I can see that he feels an urge to speak, but of course he only speaks Korean while I speak none. I wish I could speak to him. How could I speak with him? I ask myself. It is so frustrating to be restrained by just a matter of words. When will I ever again have the opportunity to be in North Korea, interacting with people of this country?

Then he looks right at me. He takes up a piece of paper and a pen. He starts drawing emergency shelters and speaking to me in his language. The translator can see us, but he doesn't even bother about our attempts at communication; I think he's tired and so is everyone else. The only thing for me to do is to continue speaking in English in response to his efforts to communicate, with words I can't understand supported by his earnest drawings.

We have a conversation about the design of shelters, the setting of camps, and where to install water points and latrines, among other things. We go through the international standards for shelter dimensions, the distance and location of facilities, lighting and safety considerations.

All of these topics we speak about, as if we can understand each other's foreign words.

We speak until the other groups finish and we are called for final plenary. We now have five or six sketches of emergency shelters. And we are both grinning. Our huge smiles come from the satisfaction of connection, of overcoming limitations and stepping into our passion. I am thrilled to share this unique moment, and I suspect he is, too.

***

At times like these, national identity falls away. He was not Korean. I was not French. All that mattered was our humanity, our common and bonding humanity. Differences were not relevant; for a moment, prejudices ceased to exist.

Interacting with the engineer in North Korea was similar to my experience of sharing coffee with the Colombian woman. In both scenarios, words were not of use. Even when cultural, political or linguistic differences present wide gaps, there is always a space where we can meet. This space is created when we are living our legacies, armed with our purpose, focusing on what matters rather than what there is.

This North Korean engineer taught me some of the key components of living your legacy:

Step into your cause

Our joint passion was protecting lives. I am no architect, much less an engineer, and he was not a professional humanitarian. Yet, we both vibrated and felt alive when our mission was saving and protecting lives. We found each other besides our differences, because we connected with what was common and real. The lesson? When we are into our purpose, we will attract people, opportunities and resources.

Ready, Fire, Aim

Ready, Fire, Aim. I like this expression used by many business experts. More than just a catchy phrase, for me this expression has become a guiding mantra in my business development. I remind myself of it regularly when I need an injection of drive or a renewed sense of direction. The usual expression says "Ready, Aim, Fire" but successful companies showed than firing and then aiming would actually lead to action and growth.

The "ready" stage is when you map out what is necessary to reach your goal. The "aiming' phase is where many get lost. I did, so many times. This is when you want everything perfectbefore launching into action: the logo, the flyer, the structure, etc. Have you experienced this in your business or your project? How has it ended? In a failure or delay to take action, right?

In our lives, this hesitation happens, too, like when you wait for the perfect time to have the baby, or when you postpone a decision, waiting for unfettered clarity before taking action. The thing is, there is no perfect moment for anything; waiting for such a moment means you risk delaying living your legacy.

After getting "ready", just fire. Gather the essential resources for taking action and go with what is available. That day in the workshop, all that was available was a piece of paper and a pen. Take your resourcefulness under your arm. Don't wait. Make it happen.

Even if you don't fully understand the nitty gritty, technical details, you just go for it. Don't postpone – later will be too late. Living your legacy is in the now, in the small and the big moments. It means stepping in with all your color, clarity, cut and carat. There will never be a better time than now to act.

If the engineer had waited, the meeting would have concluded, and the opportunity would have been lost forever. He had an opportunity to speak and share and discuss, and he took it. He "fired". He knew he didn't have the ability to communicate with me through language, so he went with what he had. He seized the moment.

The third stage is aiming and adjusting — correcting the mistakes. Sometimes that involves making big changes and maybe even feeding your "ready" phase for the next step or initiative. In this example, it could be that next time, I could turn towards a bilingual person and ask for support in translating, to get more juice out of the discussion and to create a deeper connection with future opportunities for more.

How can you translate these lessons and tips into your aim toward living your legacy at another level and with increased awareness?

We have identified our color, clarity, cut and carat. We have hints on how to start speaking your legacy. So, let us now look at the next steps to live in accordance to our purpose and legacies.

You may already have hints on what your legacy is, living it through your work or any other engagement you have, You may, on the contrary, experience that your main activity is not the place where you would like to be, but you do not know how or where you will feel aligned and into your purpose.

The first step, then, is to write down what your cause is

If you have not yet identified it, take a moment of calm and inner reflection. Close your eyes, breathe in and out through the nose. Nothing is going to come up saying, "Hello, I am your legacy," though. Release expectations.

Be free. Flow. When you breathe in, your belly inflates like a balloon. When you breathe out, your belly empties of all its air and goes inwards. What are the issues or problems that touch you most in your life, in the world? What are the opportunities you see in your community or in business that you feel frustrated no one takes advantage of?

What is your own unique crazy idea you parked on one side of your mind? Connect with this inner thought or call. Don't let the mind get in the middle. Don't worry about what others would think, or if this is relevant for you or not.

If you already have clarity on your cause, take also this inner reflection moment to clarify it and to visualize what the upgrade could be, or to identify the next level.

In the spirit of "Ready, Fire, Aim," go with what has come to your mind and your heart. Remember, you always have the opportunity to change or adjust.

The next step: Ask yourself how you will mobilize your inner diamond for your legacy

How will you put these qualities fully at the service of your legacy? Frame the answer to this question into goals, an action plan and a schedule.

I use a very simple template for this.

- S.M.A.R.T. goals – as much as possible – Specific, Measurable, Achievable, Realistic and Time-Bound.
- Based on your goals, list the required actions to be taken, prioritise the order, and specify how you are going to get them implemented.
- Schedule – all spiritual masters and business gurus will tell you that what is not scheduled does not happen. Have you experienced this yourself? I have!

Epilogue

My emergency shelter colleague gave me a sincere hug when we left the workshop room. It surprised me. Why had I assumed that North Koreans would not hug?

We smiled at each other and held hands, knowing that we would never meet again but that we felt immensely grateful for this precious, unique moment.

You can experience these types of moments only when you surrender to the magic of life — when you dare to uncover your inner diamond, even unconsciously, and when your legacy is your life journey.

If someone had told me I would come to understand the essence of living your legacy in North Korea, I would have seriously doubted it. When I landed and all seemed so different – almost surreal to me — I could not think that I would experience a major life breakthrough there. It was too far from my reality. But maybe that is just the place that we need to reach — a little distanced from our daily reality — to dare dreaming, living and embodying our legacies.

Remember:
When your life seems to be a movie set, you may not
be in any fiction but rather in the midst and the depth
of living your legacy.

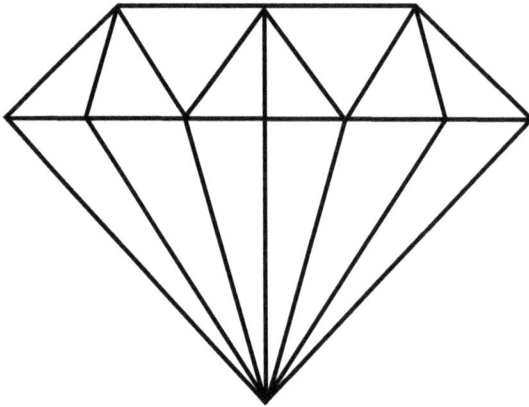

CONCLUSION

"We did not come into this world to make our lives
a comfortable sofa to fall asleep on. We came to leave
a mark. When we opt for ease and convenience, for
confusing happiness with consumption, then we end up
paying a high price indeed: we lose our freedom.
We must defend our freedom."
Pope Francis

Whenever you feel tempted to keep your diamond in the safe, when you start to believe you are only zirconium, when you feel compelled to dull your own shine, when you find you have stopped speaking your legacy, close your eyes and remember the people in this book who touched you the most — the North Korean engineer, the Afghan senior civil servant, the Cameroon businessman, the Bosnian mayor, The Guatemalan baby or the Colombian coffee maker.

Remember their wisdom and inspire yourself to speak and live your legacy, no matter what.

I plan to send a copy of this book to Adam and my Afghan friends because I know how to reach out to them. My heart believes my Guatemalan baby knows he is an inspiration for me and for you.

Maybe the others will read or hear about it, too, and contact me one day. I would like so much that each of the protagonists of the stories I shared know how they have impacted my life — and now your life and the lives of many others. I would like them to know how big their marks have been, just by being truthful to who they were.

The legacy I envision for myself is to mobilise twenty million people to speak and live their legacies. What is yours?

Your legacy is who you are, what you do and how you choose to live. The true conclusion of this book is declaring what you will set forth to do — something only you can decide. I have invited you to speak and live your legacy, and now I invite you to write it in this book: Who do you want to be? What will you do? How will you do it?

Let the words you use to respond on these lines be the beginning of living your legacy:

_____

_____

_____

_____

_____

_____

_____

_____

_____

_____

_____

_____

_____

_____

_____

_____

_____

_____

_____

Together we can shape a world where
we can all Be. Become and Belong.

Thank you for joining me.

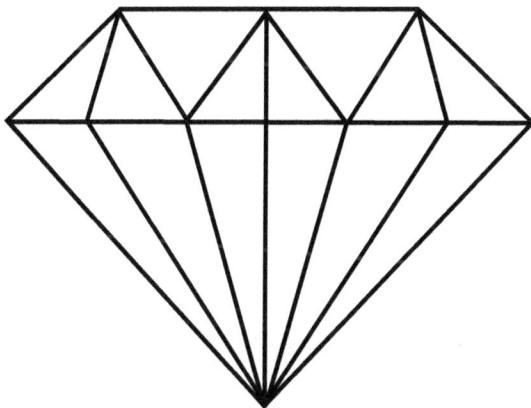

Gratitude

To myself.

When Snoop Dog received a star on the Hollywood Walk of Fame, he thanked himself for believing in himself, for working so hard, for daring and doing. This was a very inspiring moment for me and a precious reminder to thank this person we always forget to thank.

I thank myself for never giving up, for making it happen, for studying and learning , for heading higher always, even when the comfort zone is so tempting, for being grateful to those who support and forgiving to those who injure consciously or unconsciously.

To my boys.

For their patience, their love, their understanding, for all of what and who they are, for every moment. Thank you for the privilege of being your mother.

To my mum Joelle and my stepfather Laurent.

For being my emergency rescue team, when I am down, when I am traveling, when I need urgent advice, everywhere and every time.

To my brothers Antoine and Yves.

For their support, for the inspiration they give me, for being fabulous souls.

To Pedro-Luis.

For being here always, even when at the other side of the world. We married, we divorced, and we are family. And this is precious and priceless.

To my angels.

For supporting me no matter what: **Michelle Chedotal, Madhu Nagrath, Emmanuelle Bourgois, Clemento Cho, Vishwesh Chaudhari, Saratha Ramanan, Alice Carrion.**

To my soul sister May-Thanyasiri Deeying, for the unique journey we have walked together and what is yet to be walked.

To all the riders on this book-writing journey. I would like to share the story of this book – to thank all those who lived their legacies and enable me to live mine and for inspiring, maybe, those who would like to "write and live their legacies".

I remember my friend **Thierry Tardy** planting the seed of this book in my soul when he once said to me, "You should write these stories; I would love to read them." This was many years back, and yet I remember it vividly.

The idea then germinated, thanks to **Jean-François Cousin**. We had regular little catch-up lunches habits at *Broccoli Revolution* in Bangkok. I was privileged to listen to the excitements and challenges of his first book journey with his book, "Gamechangers at the Circus." That was so inspiring and gave me a lot of dos and don'ts for what I was wanting to start.

I registered for the "So You Want to be an Author" workshop by **Phoon Kok Hwa** and **Andrew Chow**. This was June 2016 in Singapore. It was an amazing two days of work and inspiring co-participants from who I am still learning and getting the support of in our WhatsApp group. A number of them are successful published authors now.

I am not very sure when I decided I would write the book but as soon as I did, it was clear that it would be in English and that I needed a writing coach and mentor as well as an editor. This was the easiest part. I knew her already: **Shannon Frandsen,** who had been the chief editorial of the magazine Wanderlust in Thailand that I was writing for. I had always been blown away by her ability to transcribe and report on topics and people with so much accuracy, honesty and sensitivity. I loved how she would correct my writing because it was always honoring who I was and what I wanted to say without judgement. There was no doubt it had to be her. And she accepted to coach me and guide in producing my first written baby.

I started the serious writing in **Sarrah Sammoon's** study room, in her Sri Lankan home where she, her husband **Armil Sammoon** and her daughter **Savaira** welcomed me for three months in 2017. Sarrah, a soul sister, an inspiring woman, a fabulous businesswoman and a literary beast. Watch her name and her daughter's: they are future best-selling authors. And her husband, a gemologist and gems trader: what a perfect environment and inspiration to write about inner diamonds. Sarrah believed in me, and she believed in my book even before I was really clear about what it would contain. She introduced me to famous Sri Lankan author **Chhimi Tenduf-La,** who generously gave me tips, resources and the encouragement to move forward.

In February 2018, it is in Landévennec abbaye by the fireplace that I wrote the most. The retirement, the prayers and the enlightening discussions with **Frère Jean-Michel** about Jesus, inner diamonds, legacy and life were fueling the drive and the inspiration.

Few months after, I sent a message to **Danijela Bogdanovic**. I wanted to check on the accuracy of my Serbo-Croatian quote in the book, and it was a gorgeous excuse to connect after so many years and to remember that both of us had envisioned a road trip through Bosnia and Serbia, still pending.

I started having "uplift" calls with **Nathalie Martin**, a beautiful coach, author and businesswoman whom I met at a conference in Paris where we both spoke. We connected so much that we decided to get on a regular call to update, support and learn from each other on this path we are both walking to reach out to as many people as we can with our message. For us it has been a sort of private mastermind that has become a must. This support is essential in the lonely journey of book writing.

In 2019, well re-settled in Madrid, I joined a few sessions at Madrid Writers Club lead by **Sean McLachlan**. It had a huge impact on my writing. I learned how to describe. I listened to other authors, and I was so lucky to be one of the Beta readers of Sean's book "Writing Secrets of the World's Most Prolific Authors."

A book is a writing journey of course – and it also requires the drive, clarity and perseverance which a successful entrepreneur needs to have.

This is what I would get by joining M1 Mastermind and Mentoring program by **Rock Thomas**: learning about goal setting and achievement, getting accountability support, developing massive action plans and keeping the mindset on a high. He is a superstar, and he is so accessible. He connected me with **Michele Budka**, a successful author and editor. She generously took time to read my book. Her advice to me that my story was "so good" that I might be able "to secure a publisher to publish traditionally" will mark the no-turning point and give the extra recharge of faith I needed.

Thanks to M1, I got mentoring advice from **Carolyn Colleen**, inspiring author and businesswoman, guidance and encouragement from my Canadian soul sister **Annette Sharpe**, fabulous coach and Chief Culture Officer at RockThomas, advice and recommendations by successful and generous **Jamie Gruber** . I met **David Simpson, Chris Hunt** and **Eric Garnicky,** who became not only business accountability partners but also a family. Each of them is really unique and left such a special imprint on my life. They are the ones guiding me, cheering me up, reminding me of my commitments, teaching me things about which I have no clue, and they are the first to trust that "Speak and Live Your Legacy" will become a bestseller.

Franck Fougère, the best in intellectual property and someone with whom I have worked on a number of projects and more to come, gave the cherry on the cake with registering the book at US Library of Congress and enabling me to add a Ó by Speak and Live Your Legacy.

Before being born, this book already counted with the best Godparents ever. I want to thank them very warmly for their foreword and reviews. I feel very honored they enjoyed the book. **Kundhavi Kadiresan,** a leader you want to be. Daring to have a vision, pushing for change even when *status quo* would make her life easier, committed to a world where we make a difference and where sustainable development goals are reached. I have been instantaneously fascinated by her. **Rock Thomas**, fabulous mentor as I mentioned earlier and so instrumental in my journey to becoming the catalyst I want to be. I do not know him physically at the time I am writing this gratitude chapter, but he is one of the most important persons in my life right now. **Anggun**, an inspiration at personal and professional levels, and a living expression of inner and outer beauty reunited. A beautiful voice and a composer: a true and authentic artist. She is the sister you want to have, the friend you want to share your joys and sorrows with. **Fred Mouawad** is at the head of a huge business empire and yet the most accessible person you can meet. His diamonds are on the crown of Miss Universe 2019 and you are blown away by the radiance of his humility. A blessing to know him. **Kamal Kishore,** a dear friend of many years, from "my" world of disaster management, a beautiful soul and person committed to people's lives. The way he has unleashed and developed his art – sketches - over the last years, inspires me so much. I am his first fan and I am so touched he has drawn a sketch for this book.

There are many **persons** I have met and talked with about the book, and their conversation and interest have boosted my spirit and my drive. There is no place to mention all but my heart sends a warm "Thank you".

I confess I am feeling a little anxious I may have missed people that had their imprint in this book. But I trust other opportunities will unfold to give me this possibility.

For the last part of gratitude, I would like to share **a poem**, by Margaret Fishback Powers, "Footprints in the Sand."

One night I dreamed a dream.
As I was walking along the beach with my Lord.
Across the dark sky flashed scenes from my life.
For each scene, I noticed two sets of footprints in the sand,
One belonging to me and one to my Lord.
After the last scene of my life flashed before me,
I looked back at the footprints in the sand.
I noticed that at many times along the path of my life,
especially at the very lowest and saddest times,
there was only one set of footprints.
This really troubled me, so I asked the Lord about it.
"Lord, you said once I decided to follow you,
You'd walk with me all the way.
But I noticed that during the saddest and most troublesome
    times of my life,
there was only one set of footprints.
I don't understand why, when I needed You the most, You
    would leave me."
He whispered, "My precious child, I love you and will never
    leave you
Never, ever, during your trials and testings.
When you saw only one set of footprints,
It was then that I carried you.

Thank you for carrying me always.

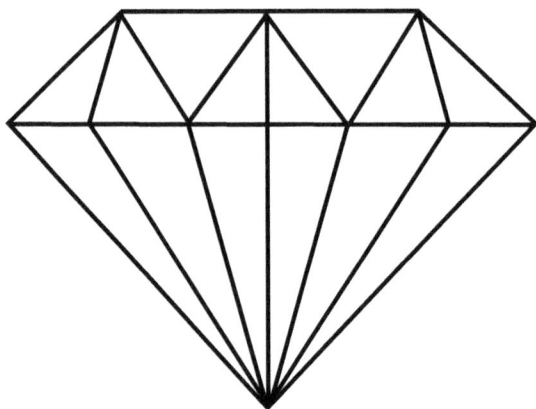

www.ingramcontent.com/pod-product-compliance
Lightning Source LLC
Chambersburg PA
CBHW071816090426
42737CB00012B/2104